T0027158

An Introduction to Veganism and Agricultural Globalism

AN INTRODUCTION TO
VEGANISM
& AGRICULTURAL GLOBALISM

Omowale Adewale

Lantern Publishing & Media • Woodstock & Brooklyn, NY

2022
Lantern Publishing & Media
PO Box 1350
Woodstock, NY 12498
www.lanternpm.org

Printed in the United States of America

Library of Congress Cataloging-in-Publication information is available upon request.

Table of Contents

PREFACE

This book was conceptualized as a helpful way of navigating veganism—whether you are embarking on a spiritual path, have come to a morally conscious conclusion, or have found that veganism is the ticket to a healthier planet. Reading this book is your choice, just like your decision to choose what you will eat for breakfast, or whether or not to receive your driver's license. However, your choice does not necessarily make you devoid of consequences or criticism or serve as your personal pass—nor can you hide behind the status quo for sanctity or refuge. Respect your choice. Be responsible and accountable for all your choices.

While, I've tried consistently throughout this book to address some of the key questions prospective and struggling vegans tend to encounter in general (such as B-12, protein, GMOs, soy, and other vegan concerns), I have not been interested in defending veganism. I believe a vegan lifestyle is its own defense. Nonetheless, in this second edition, I could not resist to highlight bees for their loyalty to the land and humanity. Bees offer so much to human beings, beyond food, and we thank them for their creation and nourishment by becoming addicted to the only food they defend at all costs—honey. We have a parasitic relationship to bees, like we do with many other animals. Bees feed us exponentially through a myriad of plant foods, while we jar their honey and their precious royal jelly designed to determine their next queen and keep their system intact. Humans destroy the authentic queen bee and install a false dummy queen in the hive to produce honey for humans, in the process contributing to the decline of bees and the degradation of our planet. A large part of this book deals with gluttony: global food systems, capitalism, supranationalism, and the so-called Third World or nations crippled by Western imperialism. I could not escape the influences of my international travels in discussing veganism or my basic understanding of world economics as it relates to all beings—*everything is political.* To ignore the external system of how we interact as agriculture consumers in the global market would seem almost unconscionable given my own history in local politics, the state of food and agriculture in the U.S., and the way in which I come in contact with resources cultivated by other human beings and animals. If there are solutions regarding compassion for our animal friends, then there must be solutions for all our human fellows worldwide, lest we all perish together.

With this second edition by Lantern Publishing & Media, besides cleaning up material and creating a shorter piece of work, I set out to add the successful Indian farmer protests of 2020 and 2021 during Covid-19. I also added a recipe and updated my biography to include Black VegFest and Liberation Farm. In addition, I wanted to highlight a handful of Black farmers and vegans in the U.S. This book is intended to supplement scholarly research in food and land sovereignty and aid new vegans.

INTRODUCTION

After I had been vegetarian for 20 years (since 1994), I became vegan in April of 2013. The process of becoming vegetarian was fairly simple. Although I had stopped consuming cow's milk, I was still having eggs and other dairy products, including cheese. I felt that was needed to satisfy my appetite. However, I had never conceived I would become vegan. I remember, maybe 18 or 19 years ago, by happenstance, looking up veganism in the dictionary and realizing that it meant I would have to refrain from dairy and egg products, as well as any other animal products. My discipline had not reached that level of commitment, and health was my main reason for going vegetarian. Doing less harm to animals was secondary to me. In retrospect, I did not know what was happening in the dairy and egg industries.

Nine years ago, I made the switch to veganism after a radio talk show host asked me in between segments why I was still a vegetarian. The direct conversation conjured up defenses, but I did not utter a word. I thought it was a reasonable question to ask since I wasn't consuming eggs, or even much dairy, by then. I knew I could easily give up dairy and eggs, so it was just a mere formality. After linking the information together, this quickly became more about animals for me. I discovered I didn't need dairy and eggs to satisfy my appetite.

I learned a simple vegetable medley could be the answer to my hunger pangs. Whether trying to lose unhealthy weight or attempting to absorb the right amount of antibacterial nutrients to prevent illness, something as simple as adding garlic and onions can be the base of a stove-top preparation. By adding some hearty chunks of sweet potato and carrots, I found I could create a nice sauce to serve over a bed of basmati rice. I was healing my hypertension, enjoying my meals, and creating different sauces, for which there are a million of combinations.

If you find yourself going vegan due to health or environmental reasons, remember it will still greatly impact animals in a most positive way. Understand that we are accountable for what we eat, but that no one's transition is the same. The injustice of consuming animals may evade some and not others. While the book centers on the human species, this vegan and agriculture discussion may greatly aid all animals.

One cannot accurately describe veganism, which involves both agriculture and environmentalism, without explaining the dangers of imperialism, the problems of capitalism, and the privilege of the West. It would be a great disservice to the average farmer abroad and those at home. After all, going vegan tends to mean eating more farmed produce.

The market around the corner is interconnected in a weblike structure with the national and global markets. It would be a catastrophic injustice to concern myself with the locality of racial justice here and not the justice of the international community. Vegans in the United States often miss the international perspective—the injustice imposed upon the farmers overseas. Ironically, the Sri Lankan farmer does not have anywhere near the dependency on animals as we do in the West.

In the simplest terms, we live in a parasitic economic system that needs resources and commodities from other developing nations. Just as abhorrent as the history of the first African being traded to initiate the financial intersection of Wall Street's pain-for-profit system, there exists a similar integral piece of the equation in producing pork commodities in that same marketplace. The compressing of the world's nations together for the benefit of Western countries is globalism.[1]

Somewhere, hidden in between appetites and dreams, there exists global compassion, even in the West. This text will provide a glimpse into the global vacuum that has disconnected the average Western inhabitant from the people of nations crippled by imperialism. This can be understood simply by linking our supermarket visits to the bananas and avocados that we love so much. Globalism is providing every fruit and vegetable in our favorite grocery store that is highly unlikely to have been grown in the U.S. Capitalism is learning that corporations use strategies to stretch their profit margin, such as adding insidious ingredients like high-fructose corn syrup to our pancake sauces, ketchups, frozen foods, sodas, and baking mixes. Imperialism is the outright theft of the aforementioned products in the form of raw materials from developing nations.

FOOD SOVEREIGNTY UNDER THE UNAPOLOGETICALLY BLACK FRAMEWORK

This section was added to the second edition to provide context to Black veganism in the spirit of food and land sovereignty. Black culture requires an elevation of thought and practice, because without thought to Black liberation, all Black culture is either consumed by the colonizer's appetite or overshadowed by the dominant culture, if not ignored entirely or in some part. So, in Black culture, it is imperative that we utilize an Unapologetically Black framework.

If we utilize the Unapologetically Black framework to explain veganism, we might identify the foods that are associated with our history of growing plants, such as watermelon or black-eyed peas. This is prior to slavery. East and Central Africans grew

1

collard greens, squash, and numerous grain cereals for several millennia and prior to the Middle Passage. Without that history, it is difficult to make the connection to operating farmland or eating only vegetation.

Utilizing the Unapologetically Black framework also explains why Black people consume foods like pig intestines or oxtails, which would have been historically discarded everywhere, including Africa. What we ate during slavery were the remains given to former slaves by white plantation owners or white stewards overseeing us in fields. These dishes made from animals were forced upon us. They are not foods uncolonized Africans would have eaten. Without this understanding and history of food, Black people have made a legacy of curating foods with sufficient seasoning to mask the putrid smell of decomposition. Not to mention that the animal foods named are low in nutrition, heavy in fat and cholesterol, and destructive to our colon. This Unapologetically Black framework is necessary for a sociological or political research, and it is also the basis for our liberation, not excluding reconnecting to African culture.

Being Unapologetically Black in the United States in food spaces is so much about establishing cultural boundaries for Black people to thrive and share communion. We all know that national origin, language, customs, and foods help us establish culture or who we are.

Black people can trace back our history of veganism some 60 years after the Emancipation Proclamation. In the purest practice of Rastafarianism, beginning in the 1930s, Rastas did not kill or consume animal flesh for food. Rastas today eat foods like callaloo, ital stew, dumplings, grains and legumes, and various root vegetables. Since then, Black veganism had been popularized in our community by health educators like Dr.

Alvenia Fulton in the 1950s, Dick Gregory in 1960s, Queen Afua in the 1970s, and folks like Dr. Sebi and Tracye Mcquirter in the 1980s and 1990s, respectively.

The Black community resonated with our food educators and healers because they were accompanied by cultural and historical food knowledge. The message of no meat did not seem foreign 50 years ago when Dr. Fulton treated residents for ulcers, heart disease, and other illnesses on the South side of Chicago, because she was communicating on the dial of Black health transformation. Dr. Fulton understood why we migrated from the South to urban centers in the North and why we needed to eat better.

However, much of the vegan mainstream messaging that enters the Black community is aggressively self-righteous and arrogant. And that in and of itself curtails Black food and land sovereignty daily. It is done so with billboards and ads we cannot afford, commercials we cannot purchase, or labor we cannot finance consistently, because we do not possess the capital necessary or the business allyships that deem our cultural needs worthy. Often, the business and finance worlds explain it as poor business and finance skills, instead of racism.

However, it comes in the form of white-led foundations and brands funding white-led vegan organizations that express in their proposals they are capable of organizing Black communities to go vegan. Meanwhile, the community feels punished, instead of supported.

This also comes in the form of high denials by banks in the U.S. During the Covid-19 pandemic, Black applicants were denied mortgage loans 84 percent more than white applicants.[1] This is the difference between quality access to food and resources during a supply shortage.

In 2021, Black farmers were denied by the USDA at a rate of 42 percent, when their white counterparts were at just 9 percent.[2] This data is consistent with why Black farmers are able to produce food on only 1.7 percent of US farmland, which is down 0.3 percent when compared to 1920. In contrast, white farmers produce food on 94 percent of US farms.[3] The data is indicative of systemic racism in the U.S.

It became crucial that Black VegFest addresses veganism and food and land sovereignty for Black people simultaneously, because our community suffers from poor eating and lack of control of our food. Why not control the food in your community? It is culturally justifiable to have good standards of food quality and evict constructs that deny community control or access. Food and land sovereignty in Black hands is about our community establishing food systems that would actually benefit Black people culturally and nutritionally. Black VegFest is an Unapologetically Black vegan festival founded in 2018 as thought put into practice that addresses the food ethics and needs of our community as it relates to food sovereignty. Members of the community experience the problem and design goals and objectives to correct them.

An example of elevated thought and practice is the struggle of Indian farmers for food and land sovereignty in recent times. After the U.S. and Monsanto and other biotech firms were linked with the neocolonialism of the Indian government, the heinously parasitic seed law was enacted. Neocolonialism is failing to address your People's struggle, while adhering to the colonizer. The reasons can be many. This relationship gave rise to an increase in farmer suicides. Many Indian farmers had their land repossessed or dried up due to big agribusiness. However, during the last 20 years, Indian farmers learned from their horrific past as colonial subjects with high suicide deaths, and they organized tighter coalitions and enhanced their communications using social media to their advantage to create the largest protest. After a powerfully defiant full year, the farmers were able to have the three farm laws repealed.

When I discuss the struggle for food and land sovereignty, it is part of the struggle for Black liberation. Black cultural foods, farming Black land, Black access to healthy healing foods, and Black veganism are all part of Black food and land sovereignty. As much as our progress is about creating individual opportunities to grow and solve our problems, Indian farmers could not have accomplished their victory without unity—Indian unity, ethnic unity, caste/class unity, and unity of liberation. The purpose of the Unapologetically Black framework is so that the individual is not commodified by the colonialist framework.

1
HEART DISEASE, OBESITY, AND FAST FOOD

Between late 2012 and 2015, I have collected research data on breakfast with a simple set of questions and answers with young people I've encountered in the Grassroots Artists MovEment (G.A.ME) and the youth program Rallying, Educating, and Building Effective Leadership (R.E.B.E.L). There has not been a controlled group, consistent quantitative data, or thorough follow-up to retrieve new data at the time or for future study, so this is significantly less of an epidemiological study and more of an awareness study. Nonetheless, I've gathered some key information and insight about youth from 14 to 22 years old living in Brooklyn, Queens, and Manhattan. The population of youth was predominantly Black and Brown. Some youth was white, Indian, Arabic, and Asian. Almost half of these young people encountered entered the program through several different larger organizations that work specifically with adjudicated youth through Alternative-to-Incarceration programs. The other half was of the same aforementioned boroughs. It should be noted that some participants were seen once and many others infrequently. My questions were simple and straightforward.

It was my task to help young people to examine their personal health choices. Also relevant are "the roles that historical and societal racism and racial and ethnic bias play and have played in creating and perpetuating these destructive and intractable health disparities...they are real, oppressive, onerous, and persistent," said Dr. Milton Mills.[1]

Whenever possible, but not through an organized system of follow-up, I asked one or two additional questions prior to a spontaneous discussion around breakfast and healthy eating.

The young people were asked, "Did you eat breakfast today?" If they ate breakfast, the follow-up question was, "What did you eat for breakfast?"

The highest-ranking answers were "I did not eat breakfast" and "bacon (sausage), egg. and cheese."

There were no preconceived thoughts about any of the specific answers I'd receive. Following this exchange of information and data, we engaged in a discussion about healthy eating, food, and breakfast. Gathering this simple data and information from the young participants that volunteered gave me incredible insight into how they approached food. The interactions led me to learn how better to approach this population of youth and young people in general, as well as how to counteract what I believed to be an enormous problem in the United States.

Discussions with adults reveal they love bacon, egg, and cheese on a roll as well. The inconspicuous bodega storefront advertisements of breakfast options in numerous urban areas make it prevalent. These bodegas, or corner stores, are placed conveniently throughout the neighborhood, and especially near all grade levels of school. Bacon, egg, and cheese sandwiches are one of the most popular breakfast foods for school-age youth and the fast-food addicted.

We have an obvious contradiction in the U.S. We urge young people to eat more healthy foods, while at the same time promote and make affordable foods that are contributing to our nation's epidemic—heart disease. Heart disease is the silent killer. It is the number one cause of death for US Americans.

Among industrialized nations, heart disease is the leading cause of death and disability, with the U.S. at the top of the list. Heart disease has been the reigning number-one killer in the U.S. for the last 95 years.[2] In 2014, an estimated $109 billion in medical services was spent on coronary heart disease in the U.S.[3] Every 43 seconds someone in the U.S. is having a heart attack.[4] Every year, an estimated 610,000 US Americans die from cardiovascular diseases, and 370,000 from coronary heart disease.[5]

Heart disease is the leading and number-one killer for men and women and most ethnic groups, with the exception of Asian Americans and US Indigenous Peoples, for whom heart disease is the second most common killer.[6] Last year, 26.6 million people in the U.S. were diagnosed with heart disease and 500,000 had a heart attack for the first time.[7] High blood pressure, high LDL (low-density lipoproteins) cholesterol, and smoking are among the three major risk factors for 49 percent of heart disease victims.[8] Other risk factors for heart disease include diabetes, overweight and obesity, and poor diet.

Obesity is classified as adults having a body mass index (BMI) of more than 30kg/m2. Overweight adults are more than 25kg/m2. According to the Center for Disease Control and Prevention (CDC), more than one-third of adults in the U.S. are obese. An estimated 17 percent of all children aged 2–19 years are also obese.[9] Every year, medical costs of obesity average $150 billion.[10] Non-Hispanic Black people have the highest rate of obesity at 47.8 percent.[11] In 2012, 69 percent of adults aged 18 and older were classified as overweight. Thirty-five percent of adults aged 20 years and older were diagnosed as obese.[12] Obese adolescents accounted for 20.5 percent of the 12 to 19 year–old population, 17 percent of the 6 to 11 year–old population, and 8.4 percent of the 2 to 5 year–old population.[13]

Heart disease prior to the 1900s was the second cause of death only to influenza and pneumonia, which had taken the nation's attention from anything else with an exceptional spike in 1919.[14] Influenza and pneumonia were responsible for almost 600 deaths per 100,000, which is still relatively high compared to today's death statistics. Shortly after 1920, significant notice was given to heart disease. It would take many generations before we would figure out a suitable protocol for this silent killer.[15] Heart disease became a national epidemic after 1920. Though the medical community agreed that obesity was a cause of heart disease, they could not agree on what caused obesity and thus could not agree on the proper prevention. Hilda Bruch, an authority on childhood obesity, pointed out that the breakthrough in tackling obesity was to eliminate bread and sweets. She argued that, based on research observations, "meat was not fat-producing." In 1957, Bruch wrote: "it was bread and sweets which lead to obesity."[16]

Dr. Alvenia Fulton opened a vegetarian restaurant, pharmacy, and health food store complex called Fultonia Health and Fasting Institute in the South side of Chicago in 1958. The Black establishment attracted Roberta Flack, Redd Foxx, Dick Gregory, and others. Later, in 1960, Jack La Lanne would develop physical exercise regiments and kitchen supplies to address obesity. In line with Bruch's theory, the American Heart Association adopted the low-fat diet in 1961, and in the same year the Framingham Heart Study concluded that "elevated cholesterol" was a major risk for heart disease. It wasn't until 1971 that a different theory was promoted—a theory that completely contradicted Bruch. In

1971, a vegetarian by the name of Frances Moore Lappe argued that fat produced from meat was, in fact, one of the main causes of obesity. In her bestseller *Diet for a Small Planet,* Lappe argued that a meatless planet is better for everyone in the world, particularly in feeding the world's poor.

Lappe's book and theory maintained a short stint of popularity amongst the US population. Her theory was immediately replaced by a more attractive philosophy that encouraged people to eat more fat, specifically fat derived from meat. In 1972, Dr. Robert C. Atkins published *Diet Revolution,* which was harshly criticized by the American Medical Association as fraudulent and dangerous to the average consumer for claiming that a high-fat diet of meat was the answer to weight loss dreams. Nonetheless, Dr. Atkins sold a million copies of his book in 6 months. The high-fat fad was later debunked by numerous studies. It wasn't until 1977 that the federal government warned Americans to eat less fat. To prevent further harm to the public, Senator McGovern held a Senate Committee Hearing to discuss the issue of diet and nutrition for Americans. The McGovern Senate Committee Hearing resulted in a report known as the McGovern Report on Dietary Guidelines. Nick Mottern, a vegetarian, was tasked with establishing the Dietary Guidelines for Americans.[17]

The McGovern Report on Dietary Guidelines encouraged the health industry to look more at nutrition data. At the beginning of the 1980s, Truswell and DarntonHill released "Food Habits of Adolescents," a research study on the increasing changes of youth living in the Western world.[18] Obesity became the most common nutritional disorder among adolescents. At the same time, the desire to lose weight amongst this population grew significantly. In a study conducted at Harvard University, 61 percent of the 450 girls interviewed said they dieted at some point in their lives.[19] Dieting was found to be more frequent during the spring. A similar study conducted in California, called the Huenemann's Study, reported that 46 percent of girls in ninth and tenth grades wanted to lose weight.[20] While girls reported the desire to lose weight, industries that attributed to weight gain grew in popularity.

Through promotion targeting younger audiences and innovative technology enhancing food size and decreasing cooking time, fast food restaurants like McDonald's became more popular, especially among children and teens. But as McDonald's popularity grew, so did the number of adolescents with obesity. An obsession grew among adolescents with acne vulgaris and their body figure, which at the time was the "most prevalent physical disorder" among young people.[21]

Truswell and Darnton-Hill explained in 1981: "For the adolescent a place like McDonald's has several things to offer. The food is inexpensive yet microbiologically safe and familiar. The items are the foods that adolescents like…There are plenty of fellow adolescents buying from or eating in these establishments."[22] The debate over how safe and how much fast food adolescents were consuming began to brew, just as McDonald's was ramping up its efforts in globalization.[23] McDonald's opened 2,000 restaurants by 1972. By 1982, they opened a total of 7,000 restaurants in the U.S. and 1,000 restaurants abroad.[24]

The National Health and Nutrition Examination Surveys (NHANES) found that between 1976 and 1994 obesity rose almost 10 points equally for men and women.[25] Between 1971 and 1974, obesity among adolescents was reported in six percent of the population. Then, between 1976 and 1980, obesity among this population skyrocketed to 11 percent of the nation in the 1988 and 1994 studies. Youth ages 6 to 11 also took part in this study, which found that their obese population consistently grew 7 points from 1974 to 1994. During the NHANES studies, fast food establishments increased from 75,000 in 1972 to almost 200,000 in 1997.[26] US sales rose 56 percent to over $100 billion between 1988 and 1998. Fast food is a strong source of fat, with the fat density being 40 percent of caloric intake.[27]

The years between 1978 and 1995 saw a rise in eating out, with over 25 percent of households eating snacks like potato chips, cookies, and ice cream away from home.[28] In 1970, eating away from home only accounted for a quarter of total food expenditures.[29] In 1998, almost half of all adults ate out at restaurants, and 47 percent of the family's budget was spent away from food at home. The trend of fast food or being able to order food and receive it in significantly less time than it would take your family to prepare it became more important than the food's actual nutritional value. In the same year, McDonald's accomplished building a restaurant in every state of the U.S.[30]

Certainly not all of our diseases or even our eating habits are attributed to McDonald's. Some of our problems with obesity and heart disease are behavioral. For starters, McDonald's introduced the McLean Deluxe burger in 1991, which was 91 percent fat-free, but since the public did not respond well to McDonald's advice on healthy eating and sales were horrible, they chucked the burger after a few years.[31] Some studies have shown that 60 percent of women do not participate in any form of exercise, and Black and Brown people were less likely to exercise when compared with Caucasians.[32] Nonetheless, there is a parallel between profit and poor health in the U.S. Fast food is attracting consumers and mass profits while numerous debates are going on for decades about whether fat is helpful, harmful, or less of an impact on heart disease and obesity. What we do know is, there's a marketing plan in place that's designed to encourage you to make a conscious decision with your money about food. And we know the food is not healthy.

Marketing and promotions are all about reaching new and continuing consumers by utilizing a variety of strategies in a highly competitive capitalist market. The fast food industry uses its full range of options, which includes but is not limited to advertisements on television networks, radio, billboards, print media, and in more recent years, social media. Within the last 10 years, traditional media outlets have had to share some of their marketing dollars with the internet. McDonald's routinely spends around a billion dollars to get you to eat their various fast food burgers.[33] That's compared with the USDA's 2015 budget allocation of $115 million to educate the entire nation on nutrition.[34]

A study examining television programming aimed at children found 56 percent of all advertisements were food-related.[35] Between 2007 and 2010, whites and Latino adults 20–39 years of age consumed almost 15 percent of their food via fast food establishments. The rate of Black consumption in the U.S. was just over 20 percent.[36]

To combat the steady rise in obesity, the US First Lady Michelle Obama launched a campaign targeting weight loss called Let's Move.[37] The First Lady explained that if the problem of obesity is not properly addressed, one-third of all US children born in 2000 will be obese later in life.[38]

This data has been consistent with the rise of the fast food industry. Until recently, McDonald's has been notorious for annually making higher profits than the year before. However, McDonald's suffered an $800-million loss in net income between years 2013 and 2014. This was partly due to a number of factors, including a recall on contaminated meat in China and Russia. There are also emerging competitors in the fast-food market with healthier options, especially those advertising vegan meals.

Transitioning to Veganism

Veganism is essentially avoiding exploitation of animals, including humans. It is my understanding that it is a principle of justice.

Under this adopted lifestyle, vegans avoid eating any animal products, including cow or "beef," fish, chicken, turkey, dog, rodent, eggs, non-human milk (that is not offered by animal to a human baby), honey, and other animal products that may be used in flavoring and coloring. As strict as this sounds, there are resources throughout this book and in numerous other publications.

Some strict vegans also avoid products made with or tested on animals, such as deodorant, clothing, and shoes. Vegans will also abstain from attending circuses, zoos, aquariums, keeping pets, and any activity that involves relying on animals for entertainment, comfort, and other converted human resources, such as horseback riding.

Foods to Reconsider

Any meat, including fish—the first half of this book has sufficient options for meals. You will not go hungry.

Excessive use of **sodium-rich products** and table salt—try seasonings that have 100 mgs of sodium or less.

White bread (severely lacking in nutrients)—check for whole-grain.

White sugar—try homemade fruit sugar, agave, which has a lower glycemic index.

Canned beans (laden with lots of sodium)—replace with dry beans and soak the night before; lentils and split peas cook faster.

Processed juice (sugar and addictive high-fructose corn syrup)—Drink more water.

Shopping Tips: Read food labels. Make a more conscious decision, which means be aware of what you are digesting and creating your new cells with and how you feed your children.

2
EXERCISE WITH YOUR CHILDREN

To best address obesity is to start our children off with healthy attitudes and activities by joining them in exercise. Whether we grew up exercising or not, we are the perfect role model and coach for our children. In addition to some ideas about nutritional choices, I impart some tips that have worked for me with my children, as well as with the youth I train.

I train my kids almost daily. They love it so much because it's short, results are evident, and they are filled with praise. They become the initiators. My youngest children were 8 and 6 in 2015. After consulting with your child's pediatrician, you can start as early as five years old.

We may begin with calisthenics and shadowboxing drills, which is just imitating boxing. I am still very much a bodybuilding enthusiast; however, I do not recommend children to lift weights before 13 years old. There is virtually no weightlifting regiment for my children. They may, on occasion for 30 seconds, incorporate shadowboxing with 2-lbs weights.

Every day, I try to re-examine the routines my kids follow. I pay attention to see if the routine is too arduous or too easy. Simple and comprehensible is fine. The idea is to test them and push their mental limits a bit for the purpose of igniting an early catabolic/anabolic relationship within their bodies that stores muscle memory. It should never be to drive them to prolonged fatigue. Routines should be short.

You challenge your child by starting virtually on the lowest or easiest level. If they are completing push-ups, try engaging them in one sole push-up. By making obtainable goals for your children, they learn to build their self-confidence. Congratulate them on every effort. Gradually increase the level of difficulty. If they're effective in completing one push-up a day, the next week the goal should be two or three.

My son has days where his form is questionable. If I want to train his mind to execute the correct form 99 percent of the time, I must coach in a manner where he is clear on what the proper form is for a push-up and the incorrect form he was using. In this method, I can eliminate fatigue, respiratory issues, or frustration to properly discern the next steps. Once I have found the issue to be poor posture, I'll often have him start over again. This is optional. My son can accomplish over 30 perfectly executed push-ups and 60 moderately decent ones. Form is significant to the point you are working the correct muscles and you are maintaining proper safety to avoid short-term and long-term injury. Form is not about aesthetics.

You can create a calendar for their responsibilities, which includes their exercises for the day. However, I do not because it's fine to skip the routine or the familiar program. I believe it's unhealthy to form a rigid habit equal to a military regiment. The idea of exercise is to sharpen minds and strengthen bodies, not to program. Nevertheless, if it helps your child(ren) to direct their attention towards the exercise awareness and planning, then having a calendar in plain sight is good in the beginning.

Like any job where you have a new recruit, you'll have to train them on the tasks and expectations ahead. Some child(ren) will be difficult to enroll. That's fine. Your difficulty may range from improper form and not following timetables to arguing the purpose of exercise and avoiding the exercise altogether. Be patient. That's your main task. As you reinforce training and even work out with them, which I strongly recommend, they will adjust to the guidelines without issue. Start off light and slow. Again, routines should be short.

Below is a list of safer child workouts. Have a few of these for your child after they arrive home from school, granted they've had a snack and all their school and home assignments have been completed.

Exercises Especially for Children:

- Jumping jacks
- Squats
- Wall-sit
- Jumping
- Wall push-ups
- Jogging and running
- Shadowboxing
- Sit-ups
- Tag
- Calf raises
- Jump-roping

3
VITAMIN B-12

Many new vegans often express concern over finding adequate sources of B-12 in their vegan lifestyle that was once found in their servings of animal meat in ample amounts. Vitamin B-12, or cobalamin, is necessary for human cell division and blood formation. B-12 is also important in the production of myelin, a protective layer covering our nerves. Deficiency in vitamin B-12 is very rare, but not having sufficient amounts may exacerbate multiple sclerosis, schizophrenia, depression, and affect neurological functions. Low amounts of B-12 may cause anemia, osteoporosis, and hearing loss. High-dosage shots of B-12 may be given to humans to treat depression and anemia.

Twenty-five years ago, the Recommended Daily Allowance (RDA) was 2 micrograms, according to the *Real Vitamin & Mineral Book*. The International Vegetarian Union (IVU) reports only 1 mcg, or 1/1,000 of a milligram, is necessary for men and women.

There is epidemiological evidence that indicates B-12 should not delay a human's transition to veganism, or even cause a minor headache. In addition to the low requirement of vitamin B-12, it can be obtained from bacterial sources in our everyday functioning regardless of whether consume food, such as poor hygiene. Vitamin B-12 can be stored in our bodies for 20 to 30 years, which may help alleviate the stress for transitioning vegans.

Our bodies also make a fair number of bacteria where B-12 can be used but not stored in this process.

Vegans also have access to healthy B-12–rich foods that supplement our lifestyle. These foods have a combination of active and inactive sources of B-12. Below is a list of vegan sources of B-12 and their amounts per 100 grams.

Vitamin B-12 Sources	Per 100 Grams
Nori, edible algae	32–78 grams
Tempeh, natto	0.70–0.80 grams
Yeast	0.50 grams
Seaweed	0.27 grams
Brown, Italian, and cremini mushrooms (raw)	0.10 grams
Portabella mushrooms (raw)	0.05 grams
White mushrooms (raw)	0.04 grams

Sources: Combs, Gerald F. "Vitamin B12." *The Vitamins*. 4th ed. San Diego, Calif.: Elsevier/Academic, 2012. Print.
Vitamin & Mineral Book. Garden City Park: Avery, 1990. Print.
"Vitamin B12." *International Vegan Union*. Web. 6 Nov. 2015.
USDA Nutrition Data

An Opinion on Nutritional Supplementation

For many young people, their focus is about substantial muscle gain. A lot of teens want protein options and muscle development. It may take years before vegans demystify how we obtain our protein, but I at least want to show my readers how easy it actually is.

When I was young and focused on developing muscle mass, I was first shocked at how quickly I was able to build strength and muscle in high school. The key was simply my drive and determination to look how I envisioned myself and simple strength training. I was already vegetarian when I started weight training.

However, when I turned 16, I began taking weight gainers, various proteins, creatine, HMB (b-Hydroxy b-Methylbutyrate), and other powders and drinks, which are mostly tested on rats.[1] Between 15 and 20 years old, weight training and bodybuilding was my main objective. Had I been in the same frame of mind with respect to developing muscle mass, I would have saved thousands of dollars and received better results at the time.

Supplement products and animal flesh are not the best source for muscle growth. You need proper nutrition and exercise with a good regiment. You can do one particular leg exercise and it could improve your flexibility, another to increase your speed and/or endurance, and yet another to define your quadriceps or add mass to your calf muscles. You can consume nutrients before workout and/or after the workout, or even based on different times of the day. This is all part of a system. Bodybuilders or any athlete going vegan can apply this same concept of body development by eating foods that grow your body for short-term and long-term results without the fat or harmful side-effects.

As I look back, I didn't need to consume all those nutritional supplements. It was a total waste, except for the knowledge I accumulated in learning how wrong supplements are for most people. How do I know? My body is generally slim. Gaining weight was historically a problem for me, until I found weight training. So, when I went back to fight in a competition in 2012, I shot from 155 to 1 80 lbs (to make it to the 178 lbs weight category) in maybe a few months. I didn't turn vegan until the next year, but when I did I was able to maintain 170 lbs. Considering that a fast-metabolizing athlete was running 15+ miles a week on plants and still able to gain more than my normal weight, I knew I should have turned vegan years ago. I realized that it was all about my intake of higher calories at the right times during the day and making sure strength training was a part of my routine.

4
VEGAN PROTEINS

Proteins are the building blocks of life. Therefore, everything requires protein to grow or exist. It should be noted that all foods contain protein. Yes, even fruit. But here is a list of some of the best options:

Seeds	Greens	Nuts	Grains
Chia	Kale	Walnuts	Brown Rice
Sunflower	Spinach	Almonds	Quinoa
Pumpkin	Collards	Pecans	Millet
Hemp	Chard	Cashews	Steel-cut oats
	Broccoli	Pistachio	Hemp
		Peanuts	Amaranth

Legumes	Algae	Veg Meats
Edamame	Spirulina	Seitan
Black-eyed Peas	Chlorella	Tempeh
Black beans		Tofu
Kidney beans		Natto
Green peas		
Lentils		
Garbanzo		
Soybeans		

Ninety-seven percent of the population gets enough protein, but not enough fiber. Vegans are getting 70 percent more than they need.[1]

Branched-Chain Amino Acids
(Leucine, Valine, and Isoleucine)

Bodybuilders and scientists express that BCAAs are the most important chain of amino acids in developing muscles. It is suggested that BCAAs be taken at a ratio of 2:1:1 (Leucine:Valine:Isoleucine).[2]

Vegan Proteins	Leucine	Valine	Isoleucine
Soybeans	938 mg	620 mg	580 mg
Edamame	926 mg	576 mg	570 mg
Lentils	628 mg	399 mg	326 mg
Seaweed	509 mg	362 mg	331 mg
Potato Flour	425 mg	356 mg	299 mg
Succotash	443 mg	306 mg	284 mg
Navy beans	442 mg	316 mg	273 mg
Broad beans	432 mg	274 mg	251 mg
Pinto beans	377 mg	270 mg	233 mg
Green peas	323 mg	235 mg	195 mg

USDA's National Nutrient Database for Standard Reference

Legumes deserving honorable mention for their BCAAs include kidney beans, hyacinth beans, mung beans, and snow peas. Plants and herbs high in the BCAAs include garlic, lambsquarters, jute, pumpkin leaves, taro leaves, raw kale, raw spinach, wakame seaweed, and sweet corn (yellow and white).

5
SEITAN

Seitan is one of my favorite foods. It's an Asian protein food over 1,000 years old.[1] Seitan is vegan and high in protein. Ounce for ounce, it's higher in protein than beef, chicken, or fish. Seitan is made from wheat gluten. Wheat gluten is the gooey protein substance that enables you to mold dough for your pizza or bread. After you wash out the starch in wheat flour, what's left is mostly the gluten. If you love bready foods, you already appreciate gluten.

Seitan is 75 percent protein, 14 percent carbohydrates, 8 percent water, and 2 percent fat.[2] This makes it a healthy addition to any meal or snack. While it provides sufficient amounts of minerals such as calcium, iron, magnesium, phosphorus, potassium, sodium, and zinc, it is not a good source of vitamins.[3]

I make seitan maybe once or twice a month. It lasts exceptionally long. Whenever I have a match coming up, I grab a bag of gluten and begin making a batch. Usually, I use seitan to help put on weight without overindulging in delicious vegan snacks. Seitan can be added to your vegetable stir-fries, curry stews, hot and cold hero sandwiches, or breaded and baked.

Like soy, seitan is often seen as a transition food and also an alternative to high-protein food. However, it's not a *transition* food or an *alternative* protein. A transition food would suggest that it's a jump to something better. It's still a plant food and, therefore, you're still 100% vegan if you digest it. The question of a food being an alternative source to meat provides the illusion that there is some mainstream protein source that is comparable. If so, the protein source would have to be vegan and thus cholesterol-free, low in fat, and still high in protein. In the vein of alternatives, beef, chicken, fish, and any animal product are very poor alternatives, at least health-wise.

There are some individuals that will claim to become irritated if they eat gluten. No matter how much juicy grapes and kiwis and powerful spinach and kale are as household names in the U.S., there will be those of us that dislike the feel of it on our tongues, our digestive tract, or the mere smell of it. With gluten, the industry has established gluten-free products that have increased in popularity in the recent years.

Yet, some have claimed adverse reactions to wheat gluten and anything gluten, including pizza or bread not labeled gluten-free. These individuals may be diagnosed with celiac disease. Celiac disease is a chronic digestive disease that results in hypersensitivity to the gliadin fraction of gluten.[4] The prevalence of celiac disease is less than one percent in America. Nonetheless, anyone who feels their body has an adverse reaction to eating bread foods should immediately consult their doctor.

Wheat gluten can be purchased at health food stores, food coops, or supermarkets. You can also buy wheat gluten directly from some manufacturers. In stores it runs for $8 to $10. Prepare to save lots of money. In the following chapter, I provide a few recipes on how to make seitan.

6
WALE'S FAVORITE VEGAN RECIPES & TIPS

I love adopting or borrowing new eating customs whenever I'm away from home, and sometimes I like to eat local so my tongue can chomp comfortably. Breakfast is my most favorite meal of the day and it's rarely ever missed. The reason why breakfast is regarded as the most important meal of the day is the necessity to acquire energy and regenerate new cells for the majority of your day. Here are some vegan ideas for any day of the week:

Breakfast
- Pancakes or french toast
- Fried seitan and assorted greens
- Seitan on a bagel with garlic and onion
- Home fries
- Tofu scramble with arugula
- Polenta or white grits
- Baked dumplings or fried plantains
- Rolled oats, quick oats with bananas
- Apples, berries, grapes, melon

Lunch

- Burrito with beans, greens, tomatoes, onions, and garlic
- Hearty soup
- Potato and chana roti
- Vegan pizzas with crust, pasta sauce, spinach, tomatoes, onions, vegan cheese
- Peanut butter and jelly
- Quinoa and black beans
- Kale salad with shredded carrots and sunflower seeds
- Hummus and pita bread
- Arugula and spinach salad with cashew nuts and strawberries

Dinner

- Vegan bean burgers
- Brown rice and lentils
- Stews with lots of veggies
- Sweet potato fries
- Seitan nuggets
- Sautéed carrots, corn, and potatoes
- Pasta with hearty chopped tomatoes

Trading for Vegan Substitutes

Combine ingredients and add them to the pan.

Perfect Fluffy Pancakes

- ½ banana or ½ cup of apple sauce
- 1/3 cup of tapioca
- 2 cups of unbleached flour
- 2 cups of hemp milk

- 2 tbsp of cinnamon
- 1/8 cup of baking powder
- 2 tbsp of olive oil
- Vegan butter (optional)

French Toast
- 2 thick slices of bread
- 1 cup of hemp milk
- ¼ cup of shredded walnuts
- 2 tbsp of brown sugar
- 1 tbsp of cinnamon
- 1 tbsp of Bob's Red Mill or ½ of banana

Bean Burgers
- 1 cup of black beans/red beans/lentils
- 1 onion
- 1 cup of panko
- 2 tbsp of coconut oil

Saturday Night Cake with Friends
- 1 store cake mix (non-dairy)
- 1 banana
- ¼ cup of oil
- ¼ cup of butter
- ¼ cup of soymilk

Seitan Dishes

<u>Seitan in Garlic Sauce</u>

Seitan Ingredients
- 1 cup of wheat gluten
- 1 cup of cold water
- 2 tsp of sea salt
- 2 tsp of black pepper
- 1 tbsp of garlic powder

Garlic Sauce Ingredients
- 1 ½ quarts of water (boiling pot)
- ¼ cup of garlic powder (boiling pot)
- 2 tsp of salt (boiling pot)
- ½ tbsp of onion powder (boiling pot)
- 1 tbsp of soy sauce (boiling pot)
- ½ tsp of xanthum gum or 1 tsp of guar gum (boiling pot)

Directions

- Mix all dry contents in a bowl. Slowly add cold water and form into dough.
- Place rolled dough inside a refrigerator for 15 minutes.
- Set water to boil.
- In hot water, stir in all garlic sauce ingredients for marinating.
- Remove dough from the refrigerator.
- Place dough into a fine mesh cheesecloth (contains from expanding).
- Add dough to boiling water uncovered for 30 minutes or until sauce starts to thicken.
- Cover pot and reduce heat to low-medium for 15 minutes.
- Remove seitan (keep inside mesh) from the stove with sauce and cool for at least 2 hours in the refrigerator.

Eat cold or heat up. Lasts two weeks or more.

Xanthum gum is part of this homemade dish and you may be new to it. It's totally safe when used as directed. Xanthum gum is a thickener. It's great for sauces and baking, and it's extracted from plants. You can find xanthum gum at health food stores, food coops, a supermarket, or online. In stores, it costs about $14. Do not add more xanthum gum than directed, not even half a teaspoon. It is heavily concentrated.

Spicy Seitan

Seitan Ingredients

- 1 cup of wheat gluten
- 1 cup of cold water

- 2 tsp of sea salt
- ½ tbsp of black pepper
- 2 tbsp of sriracha sauce

Spicy Sauce Ingredients
- 1 ½ quarts of water (boiling pot)
- ¼ cup of sriracha sauce (boiling pot)
- ½ tbsp of black pepper (boiling pot)
- 2 tsp of salt (boiling pot)
- ½ tsp of xanthum gum or 1 tsp of guar gum (boiling pot)

Directions
- Mix all dry contents in a bowl. Slowly add cold water and form into dough.
- Place rolled dough inside a refrigerator for 15 minutes.
- Set water to boil.
- In hot water, stir in all spicy sauce ingredients for marinating.
- Remove dough from the refrigerator.
- Place dough into a fine mesh cheesecloth (contains from expanding).
- Add dough to boiling water uncovered for 30 minutes or until sauce starts to thicken.
- Cover the pot and reduce heat to low-medium for 15 minutes.
- Remove seitan (keep inside the mesh) from the stove sauce and cool for at least 2 hours in the refrigerator.

Eat cold or heat up. Lasts two weeks or more.

Curry Seitan

Seitan Ingredients
- 1 cup of wheat gluten
- 1 cup of cold water
- 2 tbsp of curry powder
- 2 tsp of sea salt

Curry Sauce Ingredients
- 1 ½ quarts of water (boiling pot)
- ¼ cup of curry powder (boiling pot)
- 1 tsp of salt (boiling pot)
- ½ tsp of xanthum gum or 1 tsp of guar gum (boiling pot)

Directions
- Mix all dry contents in a bowl. Slowly add cold water and form into a dough.
- Place rolled dough inside a refrigerator for 15 minutes.
- Set water to boil.
- In hot water, stir in curry sauce ingredients for marinating.
- Remove the dough from the refrigerator.
- Place dough into a fine mesh cheesecloth (contains from expanding).
- Add dough to the boiling water uncovered for 30 minutes or until sauce starts to thicken.
- Cover the pot and reduce heat to low-medium for 15 minutes.
- Remove seitan (keep inside the mesh) from the stove sauce and cool for at least 2 hours in the refrigerator.

Eat cold or heat up. Lasts two weeks or more.

Seitan Gyro

Add pita bread, onions, and egg-less mayo or your special vegan sauce.

Sautéed or Stir-Fry Seitan

Add a little hemp oil, some peppers, onions, and black pepper and start a fire.

Seitan Stew

Add potatoes, collard greens, and carrots and serve over quinoa or brown rice.

Seitan Salad

Add spinach, arugula, and tomatoes.

Seitan Kale and Tomato

Add egg-less mayo, tomato, and kale.

Seitan on a Bagel

Add tofu scramble and egg-less mayo.

Wale's Curry Sauce for Seitan

- 2 tbsp of turmeric
- 1 tbsp of coriander
- 1 tbsp of black pepper
- 1 tsp of cumin
- 2 tsp of salt
- ¼ tsp of xanthum gum per 4–6 cups of water

BBQ Jackfruit Sandwiches (6–8 Sliders)

Ingredients
- 2 canned or 1 immature green jackfruit (instead of the sweet mature option)
- 1 onion
- 4 garlic cloves
- 2 bell peppers
- ¼ of lemon (optional)
- 1 tsp of sea salt
- 2 tsp of black pepper
- 1 tbsp of turmeric
- 2 tsp of chili powder
- 2 tsp of cayenne pepper (optional)
- 2 tsp of cumin
- 2 tbsp of olive oil
- 16 oz of barbecue sauce (no high-fructose corn syrup)
- 1 cup of vegetable broth
- Burger bread

Directions
- Preheat oven at 400 °F.
- Drain 2 canned jackfruits or carefully peel a green jackfruit with gloves to avoid sticky texture and cut into 1–1.5 inches (4 cups).
- Press jackfruit just until pieces begin to pull apart.
- In a pan with heat on low-medium, add olive oil, chopped garlic, onions, bell peppers, jackfruit, seasonings, and vegetable broth.
- Increase heat to medium-high for 15minutes.
- Turn off the heat.

- Add 4 oz of barbecue sauce.
- Place in the oven for 20 minutes on a cookie sheet.
- Remove from the oven and brush 4 oz of barbecue sauce onto the jackfruit.
- Return to oven for 15 minutes
- Toast buns (optional)
- Remove from oven and add greens and red cabbage (optional)
- Marinate overnight after adding the barbecue sauce to lock in flavors (optional).

Champ Muffins (6)

Ingredients

- 1 ½ cups of superfoods flour, or use teff or whole wheat baking flour
- 1 ¼ cups of coconut milk
- ¼ cup of almonds (crumbled)
- ¼ cup of cashews (crumbled)
- 4 tbsp of hemp
- 1/3 cup of raisins
- 1/3 cup of organic sugar
- 1 tbsp of baking powder
- ½ tbsp of baking soda
- ½ tsp of sea salt

Directions

- Preheat oven at 350 °F.
- Mix all the ingredients.
- Grease baking pan with coconut oil.
- Fill muffin cups ¾ of the way.
- Bake for 25 minutes.

Coconut Granola Cookies (8–10)

Ingredients
- ½ cup of coconut oil
- 1 cup of brown sugar
- ¼ cup of almond/soy/hemp milk
- 1 tbsp of vanilla extract
- 2 cups of flour
- 1 tsp of baking soda
- 1 tsp of baking powder
- ½ tsp of salt
- 1 cup of granola

Directions
- Mix together the coconut oil and brown sugar, then add the almond milk and vanilla.
- In a separate bowl, mix the flour, baking soda, baking powder, and salt.
- Combine the wet and dry ingredients, then fold in the granola.
- Roll into tablespoon-sized balls.
- Place them on an ungreased cookie sheet.
- Flatten out with your palm and bake for 7–10 minutes.

Smoothies

Antioxidant HDL
- 4 oz of oat milk
- ½ of banana
- 1/3 of avocado
- ¼ cup of goji berries
- 1 cup of mixed berries
- 4 strawberries

Coffee Nut

- 4 oz of sunflower milk
- 4 oz of coffee
- 1 banana
- ½ cup of peanuts
- ½ cup of pistachio
- 1 tbsp of raw sugar

Green Smooth

- 4 oz of hemp milk
- 1 banana
- ½ cup of spinach
- ½ cup of kale
- A small palm of mint
- 1 tbsp of hemp seeds

<u>Juicing Detox</u>

A detox is for those choosing veganism during their transition or trying to release toxins. I don't recommend 30-day juice fasts (I know they are all the rave). They just do not sustain the average body and do not assist your workouts. I would at least add a thick nutritious smoothie, if you're worried about gaining unnecessary weight during your detox:

- 2 cups of water
- 12 red grapes
- 1 pear
- 2 beets with stems
- 4 kale leaves
- 4 large spinach leaves
- ½ bunch of parsley

7
UNDERSTANDING WILD HYBRIDS

With so much misinformation about veganism and food, I thought it necessary to offer researched information on the subject of hybridization in general. First, let's put some of this incorrect information to rest swiftly. The notion that plants do not create hybrids in the wild is false. This should give some importance to genetically modified crops, especially as it relates to the necessity of pesticides or GMOs. Are plants not adaptable to inclement weather or pesky animals after generations? I do not pretend to have all the answers, but many gardeners, urban and rural, know these answers better than I do.

Hybrids exist in nature outside of human interaction or intervention. "There can be no question that spontaneous hybrids are of extremely common occurrence, and when they are recognized at all, they are described as variations of recognized species."[1] As pointed out by Crystal and Jacobs, hybrids may form in nature to battle drought or flood.[2] Hybridization between genetically distinct organisms can occur as the result of anthropogenic activities, such as habitat modification or individual translocation, but also as a natural phenomenon.[3]

It should be noted that hybrids and genetically modified organisms vastly differ. Remember that when hybrids are ushered in by human touch, the process can be accomplished by local gardeners next door. In the publication, *The History of Plant*

Hybrids, Focke discusses Gmelin's amazement at finding newly grown larkspurs in his garden. Focke details that Gmelin took his fascination further in documenting and categorizing plant species and researching their hybridization process. Focke states: "following this same thought farther, it appeared to him possible that the entire kingdom of plants was derived from a comparatively small number of originally created basic types. Holding this opinion, the study of newly formed plant hybrids naturally had for him a special importance."[4] If we think back before genetically modified organisms and the advent of globalism, it is possible for all humans to be properly nourished without technology. Think about the possibilities without biotechnology.

8

PHYTOESTROGENS AND THEIR RELATIONSHIPS TO HUMANS AND ANIMALS

For the purpose of investigating the great claims about soy and enriching our understanding of our broad food system, it is crucial that we properly familiarize ourselves with phytoestrogens and the way in which other primates depend upon them. Whether our food is whole or in part transgenic or all natural, organic or treated, our lack of photosynthesis renders us dependent upon the plant kingdom. We cannot create our own food internally.

Plants are classified into a wide range of subspecies. Phytoestrogen plants represent one subspecies of plants that we all consume on a daily basis. The two major chemical classes of phytoestrogens found in human diets are lignans and isoflavones.[1] Both classes have compounds that are estrogenic and antiestrogenic in their interaction with mammals.[2]

Isoflavones are heavily utilized throughout the world. Most humans around the world who are familiar with isoflavones learn about them through the popularity of the soybean. The US agriculture industry produces isoflavones for its protein and other properties.[3] Lignans are also a heavily produced class of phytoestrogens present in Western eating. Many learn about lignans through consumption of flaxseeds. Both of these phytoestrogens are present in our cereal grains, fruits, vegetables, and legumes.[4]

Isoflavones include but are not limited to various legumes; some of these common isoflavones are green peas, mung beans, pinto beans, red beans, black-eyed peas, small and large lima beans, and great northern bean seeds.[5] Lignans include fruits like apples and pears, vegetables like tomatoes, garlic, and fiddleheads, grains such as barley, rice bran, and oat bran, and some legumes, which include lentils and peanuts.[6]

Phytoestrogens have become a controversial topic mainly due to the high production of soybeans, which are classified as an estrogenic compound. Many have serious concerns about soy consumption and have created campaigns against soybeans and soy products to condemn their production, such as Weston A. Price. And while some researchers have argued that prostate cancer and/or breast cancer can be addressed by the consumption of soybeans, others argue that soybeans can be the source of these very cancers.[7]

Articles and social media videos have extracted the word estrogen from phytoestrogen to affix the same hormonal definition ascribed to human beings, which has led many to believe soybeans and soy products feminize men. A 2013 study in Ghana, *The Role of Phytoestrogens in Primate Ecology and Evolution*, conducted by Wasserman et al., returned interesting data in its behavioral study of primates. The study produced two views: 1) phytoestrogens provide health benefits, such as cancer prevention; and 2) phytoestrogens act as endocrine disruptors and threaten reproductive health.[8] These are the two foremost views on phytoestrogens for numerous reasons, which will be addressed later in the chapter.

Wasserman et al. explain the purpose of the study was used to postulate the hormonal activity via the consumption of phytoestrogens—more specifically, soybeans. Wasserman et al.

make an important distinction within the classes of lignans and isoflavones, which both belong to phytoestrogens. There exist more estrogenic compounds within isoflavones than lignans, which are found overwhelmingly in legumes. This differentiation is paramount because both lignans and isoflavones are a staple in the human diet, regardless of geographical location in the world. The Wasserman study essentially needed to draw a sharp contrast between all phytoestrogens and paint a parallel between soybeans and isoflavones. Soybeans have the highest amount of estrogenic compound among all the legumes.

Wasserman et al. in this behavioral study of captive animals suggest estrogenic plants are endogenous manipulators of primate hormones and their reproductive system. Phytoestrogens interact with animal vertebrae based on subjects of the Wasserman study, as well as the subjects of their supporting studies. The primate subjects were all captive vertebrates.

The behavioral study observed Colobus red monkeys living in Kibale National Park, Uganda, eating estrogenic *Millettia dura* leaves. The Wasserman el al. open-ended conclusion documented that the monkeys showed increases in aggression and mating and decreases in their grooming. Other studies found similar results.

According to Cederroth et al., when male mice in containment consumed soy, their sperm count decreased, compared to mice fed a soy-free diet. Marmoset monkeys fed soymilk had lower testosterone levels than twins fed standard cow milk, according to Sharpe et al. Female rats exposed to similar phytoestrogen plants resulted in fluctuating ovulation periods, which also affected their reproductive development, according to Hadley.[9]

Wasserman explained that there was a lack of data in their collection. They arrived at three hypotheses: 1) plants suppress fertility of herbivores as a defense mechanism; 2) herbivores involved in the study knowingly self-medicate by ingesting phytoestrogens for health benefits or reproductive success, and the plants actually release these compounds other than to deter herbivores; 3) lastly, herbivores and plants coincidentally interact, exchanging biochemicals.[10]

In their conclusion, Wasserman et al. assessed there was insufficient data, but summed up the teams' findings as phytoestrogens having the tendency and strong ability to manipulate hormones in humans. Humans are not named as participants of their study, yet isoflavones and soybeans are referred to as the main carriers of the agonists. Wasserman did not note a possible conflict of interest or state the lack thereof.[11] It should be noted that many in the dairy and livestock animal farming industry are vehemently opposed to soybeans because of its continual rise and versatility in being an extraordinary competitor.[12]

Primates have a historical and natural biological dependency on phytoestrogens.[13] To extract phytoestrogens from our lifestyle would mean disastrous effects for most primates, and not just apes and monkeys, as named in the studies. For instance, phytoestrogens are present in many plant foods universally deemed safe to consume by health educators; these are foods such as garbanzo beans, barley, and broccoli.[14]

Mense et al. explain that phytoestrogen compounds mimic the human estrogenic structure of the mammalian consumer.[15] Hence, the name phytoestrogen applies to how certain plants bind to our estrogen receptors. Before going further, note that the chemical and mechanical function is set apart from the behavioral activity. This may explain why billions of humans are consuming phytoestrogens daily and still procreating. This is an important distinction to consider. Being in possession of a basketball will not instantly give one Lebron James–like skills on the basketball court. One gets the equipment and possibly a title of basketball player, but there are many other factors before assessing the level of skill on the basketball court. Therefore, phytoestrogen nutrients will not impose the same estrogenic properties associated with humans.

Phytoestrogens encompass a large variety of plant foods in the wild and have made their way into our supermarkets, farms, and gardens. They are in a host of plant foods grown safe for us to eat every day, which include carrots, zucchini, asparagus, licorice, sunflower seeds, strawberries, and blueberries.[16] This broad base of foods cannot escape the diet of the average person's meal.

To fully grasp phytoestrogens and understand how isoflavones and lignans assimilate inside us after consumption, it is useful to examine the numerous studies within a demographic that has been habitual consumers of soybeans and soy products. According to the Adlercreutz study, the average amount of phytoestrogens consumed in East and Southeast Asia is 20–50 mg, compared to only 0.1 5–3 mg in the U.S and 0.49–1 mg in Europe.[17]

Soy isoflavone research was conducted using 35 studies in China and the West by Chen et al. to analyze the effect of soy isoflavone intake in pre- and post-menopausal women in China and the Western world. The study found there was a positive correlation in pre- and post-menopausal Chinese women for soy isoflavone and hormonal regulation, but also gathered there was no effect for pre- and post-menopausal women in the West.[18] This data establishes that plant estrogenic compounds have the ability to balance hormones, but also that there must be other relevant factors. More women in the United States have suffered from post-menopausal symptoms than women living in or emigrated from Asia to the U.S., according to Conroy et al.[19]

This multitude of epidemiological studies have shown that diet and nutrition can play a major part in the development of cancers. Cancer has been reported for decades as the second leading cause of death in the United States.[20] Breast cancer is the deadliest of all cancers worldwide, accounting for 16.81 percent of malignant cancers.[21]

Women in the U.S. are three times more likely to be diagnosed with breast cancer than Asian women, as identified by Ursin et al. Probst-Hensch et al. reported in the Mense study second- and third-generation Asian-American women being diagnosed at the rate of other American women, which indicated lifestyle was more fundamental in analyzing breast cancer.[22] Whether this is attributed to diet can be acknowledged as a possibility, but Asia and America are living differently as it relates to acquiring breast cancer.

A meta-analysis study pooling 785 epidemiological studies, containing over 23,000 English- and Chinese-speaking patients, found that the consumption of fruits, vegetables, and soy was more likely to reduce the risk of breast cancer in Chinese women, and that a high fat–content diet increased the risk of breast cancer.[23] Wu et al. disclosed that there was no conflict of interest noteworthy, because many researchers do not disclose whether such a conflict exists. In a 2013 systematic review focusing on isoflavones and soy in particular, Fritz et al. found a reduced risk of breast cancer incidence.[24] The epidemiological data provides a major shift in the understanding of the impact of soy isoflavones and other phytoestrogens. A Gikas and Mokbel study in 2005 of 21 case-control and 15 prospective studies concluded *there was no clear evidence between phytoestrogen and the risk of developing breast cancer*. A two-year study that investigated 220 women consuming 100 mg of soy isoflavones revealed no significant alterations in steroid hormone levels or menopausal cycle length.[25] The study was conducted by Hargreaves et al. The previous studies are consistent with Conroy et al. in soy not indicating any adverse effects in the 3,842 multiethnic women cohort.[26] However, the study did indicate women having an increased predisposition to cancer prevention when soy is consumed at an early age. Lignans, like isoflavones, have been regarded as extremely rich in providing helpful biochemical agents to address heart disease, cancers, and osteoporosis.[27]

Information sourced from Oregon State University explains that plant foods we normally consume on a daily or weekly basis contain substantial dosages of lignans, which include sesame seeds, curly kale, apricots, cabbage, pumpkins, poppy seeds, brussel sprouts, dark rye bread, durum, and wheat semolina.[28] These foods are consumed around the world from sunrise to sunset. Durazzo et al. have found lignan activities to be anticarcinogenic and antioxidant.[29]

Studies regarding heart disease consistently exhibit positive results, including the epidemiological study of 1,889 Finnish men for an average of 12 years.[30] Those with a high serum of lignans were less likely to die from coronary heart disease. Oregon State found that while the data was limited, the study of 75 post-menopausal Korean women with weak bone density found that they reacted positively to lignan intake, although a few other studies have not had those exact results.[31] The data is promising and useful, but not conclusive.

Mense et al. made a conclusion in her teams' meta-analysis study, *Phytoestrogen and Breast Cancer Prevention: Possible Mechanisms of Action.* They stated that it is inconclusive to determine whether phytoestrogens have the ability to reduce the risk of breast cancer.[32] Mense et al. explained that isoflavones and other compounds do not act alone in mammals. Isoflavone compounds produce an interaction with biochemicals and/or other foreign chemicals present in the mammalian body before they achieve their effect.[33] This may explain the inconclusive data regarding many of the aforementioned studies in this chapter.

The Incredible Soybean

The soybean can resemble a yellowish or white round ball, 1/3 of a regular-sized marble. When the soybean is soaked in water like other beans, it will expand to 3.5 times its size. Soybeans come in green pods, and when they're ripe for picking, they can be eaten right at harvest. This is their immature stage where they are termed edamame.

US food service, livestock farmers, and the industrial sector have long adapted to using soybeans, which are extremely high in protein and rich in oil.[34] Compared to meat, soybeans contain more protein and offer less LDL cholesterol.[35] US Americans love their protein almost as much as they love their meats.

Asia has been serving soybean foods like tempeh, natto, miso, edamame, and tofu for several millenia.[36] Most Americans do not know what miso or tempeh is, and outside of a health food center, it would be nearly impossible to find soybeans sold by themselves.

Americans do not directly eat soybeans nearly as much as Asian communities.

When processed and cooked, or served as cold cuts with comparable spices, the texture of soy emulates beef, pork, or chicken, to the average American palate. This explains why there is a significant increase in vegan, vegetarian, and vegfriendly restaurants in the U.S. These processes in the development of soy products will still maintain some of the soy's beneficial properties, but it's unclear how much since it is ultimately a very different bean, which will be discussed in more depth later.

Soybeans are special to America's farmers for many reasons. Farmers have an affinity for their soybean crops because their seeds are strong enough to withstand some degree of inclement weather, and they grow very quickly and easily, regardless of transgenic modification. I have grown soybeans. The soybeans' versatility and high protein content makes them an excellent feed for livestock. Livestock farmers use soy feed to produce larger animals compared to other feed, such as corn. This livestock fattening translates into more productivity and, thus, more profits.

Chemists, epidemiologists, and behavioral scientists are researching isoflavones and lignans, soybeans in particular, because cardiovascular disease, menopausal symptoms, breast and prostate cancer, diabetes, and obesity occur on a reduced scale in Asia, where soy products have been consumed for over 3,000 years (some estimates indicate 5,000 years).[37] The reality is, Asia is thriving off of isoflavones in their unfermented state of soybeans, such as tofu, and their fermented state natto and tempeh. The beginning dependence on soybean consumption has been a huge contrast between the United States and Asia, particularly China, where exists the largest nation of soybean consumers.

However, the West was not asleep long when there was money to be made. With a population boasting 360 million in China 200 years ago, about the size of the current US population, it was only a matter of time before the United States took advantage of the potential consumerism.[38]

The Growth of the Soybean

By World War II, the United States was already well invested in the soybean. In his statistical explanation of the protein demand, Houck documents that US soybean exports had increased tenfold between 1946 and 1961 to over 100 million bushels in whole soybeans, and a few hundred million bushels of crushed soybeans.[39] During the same time, the price of whole beans decreased by 33 percent, and the price of soybean oil dropped from 24 cents per pound to 8 cents per pound.[40] Exports were limited to whole soybeans, soybean meal, and oil. The same characteristics of importance to consumers of soy products today were similar to many at that time—versatility of usage and high protein content.[41]

The soybean commodity grew in popularity due to its various proprietary uses. Today, the soybean is understood as cholesterol-free and an ally in addressing some of the worse human diseases and illnesses in the U.S. Soybeans are a protein substitute used in veggie foods, such as hotdogs, hamburgers, granola, cookies, doughnuts, energy bars, protein shakes, ice cream, and milk.

While it is exceptionally difficult to avoid phytoestrogens, even isoflavones, I am convinced by theory and practice that it is very possible to reduce or eliminate soybean and soy product usage and maintain an exceptionally healthy life. Regardless of my personal affinity for soybeans, it is not the only crop with dietary health benefits. Plant foods associated with improving health and vitality are endless. You can eat spinach, kale, collard greens, garlic, and onions and increase your healthy bioactivity. Factors associated with health and wellness outside of choosing a proper diet are also innumerable. Just remaining calm and meditating can reduce stress levels and have positive results on your blood pressure. No one should place all their soybeans in one bushel.

9
THE RISE OF U.S. GENETICALLY MODIFIED ORGANISMS (GMOS)

How is it possible for the United States of America, less than a third the size of China, to have such a financial lock on a commodity that has been grown and eaten for over 3,000 years in China and the rest of Asia?[1] Although the U.S. has long been an exporter of soybeans to China, to satisfy Americans' enormous hunger for the high-protein food, hundreds of thousands of acres of fertile land in the Midwest have been dedicated to soybean agriculture. The American stranglehold of soybeans is due to the ambitious decision to legitimize genetically modified soybeans.

Scientists in the U.S. had been trying to achieve transgenic success since the mid-1970s.[2] In 1985, Horsh et al. became successful at the most important step in creating genetically modified organisms (GMOs).[3] GMOs involve altering deoxyribonucleic acid (DNA) belonging to a living being.[4] The transgenic approach may involve adding or removing DNA from one species for a specific purpose. This may involve one or several more radically different species.

According to the United States Department of Agriculture (USDA), genetic engineering began in 1982 with the splicing of the first potential crop, a tomato plant FlavrSavr.[5] By 1994, with US officials establishing bio-safety standards, commercialization of GMO plants was underway, albeit with heavy skepticism from around the globe.[6] It wasn't until 1996 that three major GMO crops in the U.S.—soy, corn, and cotton—would enter the food market.[7]

According to the United States' Animal and Plant Health Inspection Service (APHIS), the agency charged with commercial authorizations of GMO, the highest number of permits to biotechnical firms—a record 1,194—happened in 2002.[8] Annually, APHIS grants an average of 800 permits to biotech companies. Two years ago, Information Systems for Biotechnology reported the lowest number of authorizations granted since 1993, with only 536 permits.[9] Lower annual permit numbers do not mean less GMOs entering the market.

After years on the market, a biotech business may apply for non-regulated status. If accepted, APHIS ceases to provide oversight of the GMO plants in question. This translates into GMOs being on the market just as any other agricultural product for sale. Therefore, while the number of permits has decreased over a decade, the number of actual GMO marker plants with gene expression that the USDA has deemed constructs increased 15,000% between 2000 and 2012. The 2005 calendar year represents the largest percentage jump in authorized constructs. Constructs are GMO plants crafted in a laboratory.[10] One authorization of a single GMO plant may enable 10 gene expressions of a single marker gene, which may generate thousands of seeds and plants, and are then, in turn, sold and/or grown by farmers.

The top ten most cultivated GMO plants authorized for production, in descending order as of September 2013, are corn (with a ratio of 3:1 to the second GMO crop), soybean, cotton, potato, tomato, wheat, alfalfa, tobacco, rapeseed, and rice.[11] Authorized GMO permits or notifications for just the 10 foremost crops ranged between 294 (rice) and 7,778 (corn). The top ten most authorized producers of GMOs, in descending order as of September 2013, were Monsanto (with a ratio of 6:1 to the second GMO crop), Pioneer (now part of DuPont), Syngenta, USDA/ARS, AgrEvo, Dow AgroSciences, DuPont, ArborGen, Bayer CropScience, and Seminis. The biotech firm authorizations range from 210 to 6,782.[12]

Farmers purchase GMO seeds from biotech firms, sometimes at higher costs than non-GMOs because they are promised herbicide tolerance, insect resistance, virus/fungi resistance, agronomic properties (such as resistance to drought and frost, longer shelf life, and modified flavor or increases in nutrition). This is understood to be a tremendous benefit to farmers who are growing the aforementioned top ten products, in addition to growing squash, melon, papaya, sugar beet, other produce, and flowers.[13]

As biotechnology soared in the United States, so did agricultural output. In 2000, among the top three major GMO crops in the U.S., there were just under 69.5 million acres of GMO products planted; by 2013, US farmers had increased to 169 million acres of the same three crops. Agribusiness is currently booming.[14] Forty-one percent of all US agriculture acreage was GMO fields in 2012.[15] The saturation of GMO crops caused some to contaminate several non-GMO crops.[16]

At one point, soybeans were the top GMO crop in production among US planters. In 2000, soybeans represented 40 million acres of GMO crops, compared to corn, which has inhabited the Americas for 7 millennia, with just under 20 million acres in GMO crops.[17] This is an interesting difference in crop production, since corn continues to yield higher returns and remains the highest exported crop in the U.S.

One can hypothesize that US farmers of GMO soy may have initially been more comfortable experimenting with GMOs in China than in the U.S. before shifting over to the high-yielding GMO corn. Possibilities also include higher demands for more protein content for livestock and the increased human consumption of soybeans internationally through numerous products. The fact is that American farmers intentionally used more HT soy (herbicide tolerance) than HT corn, respective of their varieties.[18] In 2000, GMO soy accounted for 54 percent of all soy crops, and GMO corn only 7 percent of all corn grown in the U.S. By 2005, it was 87 percent compared to only 26 percent. Corn still leads all US crops in planting and exports, regardless of GMO variety during that time.[19]

The USDA reported a change in tide among the two leading US crops in 2007, with GMO corn edging GMO soy crops by almost 10 million acres for the first time in GMO history.[20] This indicated to insiders that American farmers and US companies were more comfortable with GMOs for producing greater yields of high-fructose corn syrup products and GMO cereal brands. Corn has always been the top-harvested crop in the United States, making the U.S. the largest producer of all corn varieties.[21]

Nonetheless, on a global scale, soy dominates all crops in production. The high interest among international farmers purchasing GMO seeds is acquiring herbicide tolerance, insect tolerance, agronomic properties, and high oleic acid, which pertains to the production of unsaturated soybean oil.[22]

The United States rolled the dice on the GMO soybean production amidst heavy opposition to genetically engineered foods internationally and managed to show gains almost every step of the way. Biotechnology has spearheaded the U.S. in an entirely new influential stratosphere, and that is owed to genetic engineering. In 1999, only three years after the commercialization of genetic engineering, the Federal Drug Administration (FDA) approved soy's health claim that it can reduce the risk of coronary artery disease.[23] It was almost impossible to argue against it, since soy had already been a commercial powerhouse for decades, and scientists had confirmed the claim through numerous studies. By 2010, Americans were polled and found that 84 percent believed soybeans were healthy.[24]

Immediately following this great news for farmers, the price of purchasing soybeans increased by 50 percent. In 2014, the soybean amassed $27.5 billion more in domestic and international sales than in 1998.[25] Between 1998 and 2014, the soybean harvest expanded to 82.5 million acres, a 15 percent increase. Soybeans, which were exported by the millions of bushels in the 1950s, are exported in the billions of bushels today.[26] At the end of 2014, soybeans had almost 4 billion bushels, or 120 million tons in production.[27] Exports for the marketing period of August 2013/2014 reported exports at 1.6 billion bushels of soybeans.[28] The following marketing period showed an increase of 166 million bushels.[29] This accounted for 48 countries, with China taking the majority of the shipments at 880 million bushels, amounting to $8 billion.[30]

To be clear, US genetic engineering essentially became biotechnology. Everything else associated with biotechnology was moved to the rear of the science laboratory to make room for agribusiness. The United States government began seizing upon every potential opportunity the soybean could offer. Internationally, the U.S. has invested a great deal of effort, resources, and political clout to get GMOs globally accepted. The biotech industry would not be as global and wealthy had it not been for US American influence during the last 20 years of its progress, as later chapters reveal. Of course, the U.S. is also proud of having a strong ally who believes in the same capitalist approach in helping to keep the country visible and invested in the brand of the United States of America.

Nevertheless, the biotech business is no more exceptional or pervasive than the tentacles of Hollywood. It's no more capitalist and aggressive than the sludge of the US energy industry, and no more talented than information technology creeping into your towns and villages across the world. The U.S. is global in its trade operations.

However, the biotech industry is different. It is everywhere like an oil spill, but their products cannot simply be washed away or turned off like a movie projector or a computer. The biotech industry designs products that stay within us. They are developed in a laboratory, but they manifest through the soils of the earth and envelope us and all other animals they come in contact with, and they merge seamlessly. This is a significant difference. Big agribusiness is as agricultural as it is chemical.

10

THE EUROPEAN UNION: AN INFORMED PUBLIC

The defense of genetic modification typically occurs due to the agricultural and human investment involved, as well as the political (power) motivation. No amount of money could compare to the number of farmers who have divested from non-GMO, even in the traditional inorganic way of poisoning pests. They are still biological agents developed by Monsanto, yet it is virtually impossible for most farmers to revert back to non-GMO without losing their business and their livelihood. While this could be one of, if not the largest, problem for the US labor force and agriculture industry in the years to come, the current situation for farmers is between a rock and a hard place. They must churn out GMO crops nonstop. They will need China and their historical allies in the West. Nevertheless, health and environmental concerns are front and center worldwide.

Public acceptance of the biotech industry did not incubate in a laboratory. Since 1992, the FDA sent assurances to the global public that GMOs are safe.[1] The FDA helped streamline testing and calmed fears in the U.S., to the extent that farmers began planting and distributing in 1996.[2] However, much of the world was still not confident in genetic engineering. US officials would have to usher in their international trade diplomacy tactics for the auspices of its agricultural and farming investment worth around $955 billion, or 5.7 percent of the gross domestic product (GDP), an amount grossly underrated. Agriculture and farming also relate to restaurants, weddings, catering, forestry, fishing, beverages, apparel, and a lot more. There's a direct correlation to commodities like cotton, corn, soybeans, and livestock grown in the United States (ERS USDA).

In 1994, after trade friction between the United States and the European Union over proper testing of genetic modification, the Food and Agricultural Organization (FAO) and the World Health Organization (WHO) set up the United Nations Codex Alimentarius Commission for global standards on food safety. Additionally, as another pacifying measure for the European Union and other nations around world, the U.S. agreed to the World Trade Organization (WTO) adopting the Application of Sanitary and Phytosanitary Measures (SPS Agreement).[3]

While there were several members of the EU governments open to the potential of genetically modified crops and GMO products, that changed dramatically after Monsanto's rBST (recombinant bovine somatotropin), also referred to as rBGH (recombinant bovine growth hormone), following links to breast cancer after a study conducted at the University of Vermont.[4] The FDA first approved rBGH in 1993 for farmers seeking to increase milk production by 10–15 percent.[5]

This set off a firestorm for consumers and Non-Governmental Organizations (NGOs) of the EU that were already skeptical. The EU blocked US exporters from shipping hormone-treated beef, igniting a transatlantic trade war. Erupting into an international tantrum because of EU's fear and opposition to GMOs, the U.S. referred to their WTO SPS Agreement because they said this was not based in scientific evidence. The WTO ultimately ruled in favor of the U.S., citing there was no scientific proof that GMOs were harmful to human health, environment, or animals.[6] But, international agreements being unenforceable, the general EU ban was never lifted. However, some nations chose to trade in US GMO products.

Based on GMO Compass surveillance, several EU countries have transgenic crops, including the U.K., Spain, Greece, Germany, Austria, Finland, and the Netherlands. Unlike most nations in the E.U., Italy and Switzerland have maintained a strong all-inclusive ban or moratorium on GMO cultivation, respectively. The larger part of the E.U. has a ban specifically on Monsanto's maize (patent 810).[7]

Nonetheless, from the point of view of the West, the loudest of the anti-GMO agricultural communities are located in Europe. The European Union required state approval of GMO products and GMO labeling as of 1998, which prompted a senior US trade official to state: "Europe's attitude toward GM foods and agricultural products is the single greatest threat to US agricultural exports."[8]

The most striking difference, perhaps, between food sovereignty principles and the reality of US food systems is in democratic control over decision-making related to food. On issues ranging from labeling of foods containing genetically modified ingredients to confined animal feeding operations, policymakers from the municipal to federal level have disregarded strong opinions expressed in public polls and chosen policies that favor corporate interests and lobbyists.[9]

In numerous cases, agribiotech firms have been negated in their quest to annually expand their seeds throughout Europe. Two years ago, a biotech firm BASF through its subsidiary attempted to place Amflora (potato modification) on the market and was rejected on the basis of risk to human health and the environment. Hungary was responsible for bringing the annulment, in collaboration with France, Luxembourg, Austria, and Poland.[10] Earlier this year, Syngenta, attempting to introduce four new GMO traits for EU approval, was forced to rescind two commercial biotech products, one herbicide-resistant and the other both pesticide-producing and herbicide-resistant.[11]

However, the European Commission recently attempted to circumvent the unified process of the European Parliament by issuing a proposal for some EU nations to opt out of EU authorization.[12] That proposal was harshly criticized and then rejected. In August of 2015, the Scottish government formally prohibited the growing of genetically modified crops. The Cabinet Secretary for Rural Affairs, Food, and Environment Richard Neilson Lochhead said, "The Scottish government was not prepared to gamble with the future of the country's GBP 14 billion food and drink sector" (Rhodes-Vivour). Quotes by the oldest and number one producer of biotechnology Monsanto provide a chilling reminder of what their motives are and the lack of ethical standards.[13] "Monsanto should not have to vouchsafe the safety of biotech food. Our interest is in selling as much of it as possible," Phil Angell, Monsanto's director of corporate communications, points out.[14]

The continuous rejection of questionable products by the E.U. approved for production in the U.S. is indicative of their residents' consciousness and US greed. Europe maintains controls in food safety and bends to their population's awareness. Greenpeace recently illustrated the EU residents' outrage with the signing of a petition to the tune of 2.3 million signatories to discontinue trade talks with the U.S. and Canada, citing economic and agricultural concerns.[15] This action and many others like it illustrate a sharp contrast to American behavior. In 2000, the International Food Information Council polled US Americans about GMOs and 34 percent did not know what they were. Another 23 percent didn't believe GMOs, a made-in-the-USA product, were sold in their country.[16] Basic awareness about food consumption remains to be a key difference between the U.S. and other Westerners. The U.S. is still one of the only nations that refuses to adopt labeling standards, opting to allow corporations the ability to regulate themselves. This is consistent with USA's stance that GMO varieties are consistent in the look, feel, smell, and taste with non-GMO products. From the looks of it, there is no chance the U.S. will bend on GMOs, because they are in the best corporate interest.

The U.K. and Australia, although both fully committed as liberal-trade nations and GMO exploiters, have created a host of safety standards and national labeling systems for their residents. Russia, a non-EU member and initially a supporter of at least 17 different GMO varieties, recently changed its position and vouched to abstain from conducting any more cultivation or exporting of GMO products. Russia also offered a sharp warning to the US biotech industry that threatened to bring criminal actions to any firm that attempts to plant GMO crops on Russian soil.

11

THE THIRD WORLD: A WORLDVIEW OF AGRICULTURAL TRADE

Veganism, in the sense of food, nutrition, and wellness, is the highest level of consumption. Just as Earth being the revolver around the sun and not the center, this will be debated for some time. However, its benefits of anti-aging, antioxidant, and anti-bacterial nutritional value and overall health are documented. But veganism in that US American way of thinking is incredibly limited. Veganism by itself does not address suffering, nor does it take into account its strain on global borders. For instance, as more cars increased within the U.S. over the years, so have the nation's demand for oil. The prices of oil and gasoline were raised, and we took notice. We saw that oil is not sustainable.

The way in which our food comes to our table is largely dependent upon global trade as well. The system in place also indicates this will not be sustainable. We understand this basic concept of international agricultural trade. We need foods that are grown in other climates of the world.

However, we fail to recognize it in the U.S. through the misinformation of politicians on both sides of the aisle and on the peripheries. As a result of our justifiable ignorance and bias, we negatively impact low-income, developing nations, and not just in this instance, but historically and consistently. This is why people immigrate to the U.S. or die trying. While this is no more important than our national health, sexism, racism, or speciesism, this is our health and environment in harm's way. This agricultural trade *is sexist, racist,* and speciesist in a global way.

La Via Campesina (LVC), which originally proposed the concept of food sovereignty at the 1996 World Food Summit, set forth seven principles: food—a basic human right, agrarian reform, protecting natural resources, reorganizing food trade, ending the globalization of hunger, social peace, and democratic control. These basic human rights have been formed into a demand for food security and human dignity.[1]

Since the 1920s of industrialization, the U.S. has been moving forward as a major competitor in the world. Following WWII, the U.S. has been crafting meaningful ways to stay in power. Following the agreement and formation of the 1994 World Trade Organization (WTO), every nation based on its GDP and income level was given a certain number of years to create legally binding agricultural and patent laws within their own country.[2] The time is just about up.

With the advent of genetically modified organisms and the increase in agriculture, the WTO's vague language is ever more relevant. Focusing on most of the world's continents, developed and developing nations, there have been substantial trade issues since that signing based particularly on GMOs. The following are just some of the most recent global hiccups ascribed to the administering of the articles of the 1994 WTO agreement.

Southeast Asia: India Learns from Its Colonialist History

In 2001, the Protection of Plant Varieties & Farmers' Rights Authority (PPVFR) of India was passed after seven years of contentious battles.[3] While this legislation is the antithesis of local community farming, activists managed to influence legislators to incorporate some farmers' rights, particularly those associated with the sale of protected varieties. The farmers are still able to save, use, sow, exchange, and share seeds, except for branded ones, such as those made GMO by biotech companies.[4] The rights given to the farmers were always afforded to Indian people for thousands of years on the basis of culture and land. The PPVFR law is actually an extension of the multinational WTO agreement of 1994 that helps protect US investment, with the biotech industry acting as a shark.[5]

PPVFR gives intellectual property to biotech firms. GMO plants are hazardous to non-GMO plants, and so is the relationship between farmers' cultural seeds and the seeds of big agribusiness or biotech firms. GMO seeds are currently protected by intellectual property in the West. Therefore, for instance in Indiana, if GMO pollen blows in a non-GMO farmer's yard, not only does the GMO pollen have the power to wipe out all of the farmer's non-GMO crops, but it will begin to prop up new GMO crops that belong to the company that produced the marker gene.[6]

In an open letter to Prime Minister Narendra Modi of India and US President Barack Obama, the Navdanya movement documented several cases of US biotech firms, such as Monsanto, Syngenta, and Conagra, claiming violation of intellectual patents by Indian farmers for planting and producing Indian crops in India.[7] Each of the crops is centuries, if not a couple millennia, old, such as seeds for basmati rice, Atta wheat flour, and neem, which is used as fungicide and safe insect deterrent.[8]

Physicist and Environmental Activist Vandana Shiva talked with a Sri Lankan audience in 2014, explaining the last 14 years after India adopted the PPVFR.[9] Shiva described the repercussions felt by her Indian homeland and dangers of genetic engineering in Punjab. "Punjab is one of the states with highest rates of farmer suicides. The water is disappearing so fast because the green revolution required 10 times more water to produce the same amount of food. Punjab means the land of the five rivers. Today the land of the five rivers is dry because of its excessive use of water."[10] Shiva, speaking in opposition to the Seed Law and the influence of the West on Brown nations, said:

> Farming and agriculture is something countries like India have done for 10,000 years. What we see with the biotech companies is really chemical industry. Companies like Monsanto that gave us Agent Orange (crop herbicide used in Vietnam linked to birth

defects). That is the kind of industry that is claiming
to benefit Third World agriculture. They know how
to manipulate chemicals and plants, that's not about
farming, that's not about good food. I don't believe
they have anything to give to us.[11]

Shiva outlines very clearly the problems of globalism and
supranationalism as they relate to food security and economic
survival. With three-quarters of the world relying on agriculture
for both economic and cultural sustenance, the US plan of
liberal trade is a death trap for the majority of the earth's people.
Small farmers will not be able to compete with cheaper imports.
Historically, supranational organizations, such as the World
Bank, International Monetary Fund (IMF), and the Food and
Agricultural Organization (FAO), have ushered in agribusiness
for the purpose of acquiring land and reaping more benefits
around the world.

In the world's largest protest in recent memory, 300 million
Indians protested the three farm laws enacted in 2020. Indian
activists argued foreign private businesses would systematically
crush small farmers and decrease families' access to local
commodities. Indian Prime Minister Narendra Modi announced
the repeal in November of 2021.[12] The US mainstream media
conveniently failed to accurately report the upheaval in India.
Many believe it is because Indian farmers were afraid that major
US brands would further control Indian food and land.

Sri Lanka is also under constant pressure by the UN's Food and Agricultural Organization (FAO) and the World Bank as they attempt to plant the objectives of the Western world outlined in WTO's 1994 document. Sri Lanka is faced with the same fate as India—the installation of the Seed and Plating Material Act. Farmers' rights activist Sarath Fernando with Movement of National Agricultural Land and National Reform (MONLAR) forewarn the negative effects for the farmers regarding the proposed seed law. "This kind of legislation is being pushed all over the world. It is an international plan, beneficial to big seed companies in taking control."[13] Last year, MONLAR conducted marches and mass protests in attempts to rally farmers and residents around pushing back against corrupt government and big agribusiness.

The Environmental Justice Atlas, discussing farmers' concerns with the seed law, explained farms will be raided due to the legislation, and a forced database collecting farmers' names will be instituted. To add to these depressing matters, farmers will be prohibited from seed sharing and forced to purchase "certified" seeds, which will place undue burden on farmers. Essentially, Sri Lankan government is developing a WTO law to fit into a Western design of agriculture. This is not about addressing poverty. Whether the seeds are GMO or not, biotech firms such as Monsanto and Syngenta are concerned about neutralizing non-GMO seeds and monopolizing GMO seeds, which stand to become all seeds.[14] If biotechnology wins over indigenous planting, the farmers will become serfs to the land run by foreigners.

This push in Sri Lanka is being orchestrated by the UN's Food and Agriculture Organization (FAO) and the Asian Development Bank (ADB). ADB advertises on its website that it has shifted its strategic focus from agriculture to a comprehensive multi-sector food security engagement, with the goal of curbing food insecurity, particularly among the low-income and vulnerable. The ADB further states their focus is on integrating agricultural productivity and the food market.

However, the Asian Peoples' Movement Against ADB challenged the ADB's assertion, detailing that "for more than 40 years, we have been witnessing and learning that ADB intervention has created food, energy, financial, and social crises. We have been witnessing ADB's full support to the private sector, as well as full direction to Indonesian government to follow a system that has been proven failurefree market policies. [However,] ADB debt projects have only increased the number of the poor people in Asia."[15]

Agribusinesses will eventually end up operating the land when rural farmers are no longer able to pay. Whether the farmers are muscled out or stay, the crops are there providing residual funds for biotech companies. It makes perfect capitalist sense. Farmers will have to continuously buy seeds from agribusinesses. Thus, if the intellectual property laws lobbied by biotech firms solidify anywhere in the world, the biotech firms present a significant risk to all the world's food security.[16]

Sub-Saharan Africa Becomes Influenced by GMO Foods

Sub-Saharan Africa has in the past been steadfast in its opposition to GMOs coming onto the continent for testing.[17] However, unlike Europe, their lack of economic stability and historical relationship to Western colonialism make them more predisposed to exploitative tactics by the U.S. While the practice of unwanted US businesses harassing the E.U. is bothersome, they cannot be made susceptible to neocolonialists and supranationals. Imperialism wears down the armor of their economically and politically weaker nations. However, 13 years ago, the Motherland had not been ready to give in so easy.

In Africa's moment of vulnerability, faced with extreme drought during the typical dry season, and coupled with starvation, debt, and illness, in 2002, a handful of nations shocked the Western world by imagining a future with no genetic modification. The decision by nations Malawi, Mozambique, Zambia, and Zimbabwe rejected US food aid marked by a concoction of GMO variety. It was met with Western hostility.[18] As African governments chose to make a collective decision about the future of its citizens, the U.S. with Canada, Australia, and Argentina suspected they were more influenced by Zimbabwe's unbending Robert Mugabe and anti-GMO groups in Europe.

The moment was tainted by controversy when, at the recommendation of the International Monetary Fund (IMF) and the World Bank, Malawi's President Muluzi sold off its maize reserves of 165,000 metric tons to pay a debt to the banks.[19] The lack of independence and forward thinking exhibited by President Muluzi made him fodder for the US Congress and the Western world that, in turn, pointed to his incompetence, leading many nations to cancel any debt relief to Malawi's suffering people.[20] The mere semblance of autonomy is no match for your real colonizers.

Considering the IMF's impeccable timing to make such a poor recommendation to Malawi, it is more than questionable. Southern Africa has typically had droughts during that time, and the IMF may capably discern whether it is prudent to provide a prescription for debt repayment that involved the bulk of Malawi's food resources.[21] Whether it may seem far-fetched to argue the probability of supranationals orchestrating this illegitimate recommendation to render Malawi weak and helpless, it placed Malawi directly under the thumb of the West. The same year, Malawi passed the Biosafety Policy, rolling out the red carpet for biotech firms.

Africa's strongest proponents in maintaining the distance between biotechnology and agriculture, both Nigeria and Ghana concede to Monsanto and the WTO. Two of the most powerful and stable governments in Africa have made concessions to allow a three-day biotechnology course between University of Ghana (UG) Legon and Michigan State. Both nations agreed that biotechnology is essential to food security.[22]

The Alliance for Food Sovereignly in Africa (AFSA) reported in July of 2015 that in accordance with President John Dramani Maham, the African Regional Intellectual Property Organization (ARIPO) in Ghana adopted the Arusha Protocol for the Protection of New Varieties of Plants (the "Arusha PVP Protocol"), which other nations have been approving for the biotech firms.[23] The intellectual property rights in Ghana for agribusinesses and biotech entities will at the very least destroy West African farming and take ownership over crops that are culturally Ghanaian. Biotech companies being "protected" under such legislation is not simply safeguarding rights of businessmen; protection for the biotech industry will lead to non-GMO palm trees being handed over to big agribusiness. Seeds will be collected, altered, and no longer authentically the same plant. This is the return back to colonialism and serfdom through privatization. Farmers and families will be forced to till land for a lifetime. This is what farmers are fighting against in Brazil and what is being linked to the high number of Indian suicides.

Reported in October 2015, "The Human Rights Division of the High Court dismissed the suit for interlocutory injunction to prevent the Ministry of Agriculture and the National Biosafety Committee (NBC) from releasing and commercializing genetically modified food in Ghana," lifting a longtime ban on GMO products.[24] This devastating loss by AFSA and other African organizers set up Ghana to begin producing GMO food sometime in 2016, if the plough is not already in the land.

President Goodluck Johnathan of the most populated nation of Africa signed the National Bio-Safety Bill in 2015, revealing Nigeria will be ushering in a new era of GMO crops to be cultivated on the land.[25] This is not simply corrupt politics, it's the WTO going step-by-step, installing genetic biotechnology on the shores of Africa. With this legislation, Nigeria gave the appearance of actively addressing health and environmental concerns, but to adopt GMOs is to run contrary to public concern. They are in reality marketing themselves to big agribusiness at the expense of the farmer.

Already in the pipeline are GMO versions of cotton, maize, and soybeans, the three major crops in the U.S.[26] National

Biotechnology Development Agency (NABDA) Director–General Professor Lucy Jumeyi Ogbadu said, "Signing the biosafety bill is a milestone in the domestication of modem biotechnology in Nigeria. It is a giant stride that will allow the country to join the league of countries advanced in the use of this cutting-edge technology as another window to boost economic development in Nigeria. It will create more employment, boost food production that will put a smile on the faces of farmers and elevate hunger."[27]

However, that is historically incorrect and pure exaggeration. There will be employment, but it will be in the form of sharecropping. There is already substantial evidence in sub-Saharan Africa's past. First, the latter illustrates for us that supranationals, bearing gifts of the U.S., have continued to short-change developing nations on equitable trade. This is obvious in the case of India having very few farmers increase their wealth, while the majority struggle to make a living. The reality of big agribusiness is when and where farm economies do blossom, it seems that the great bulk of the marketed surplus comes from a small fraction of farmers.[28]

For developing nations that will ignore the recent signs based on the differences of peoples and geography, the past provides further proof that Nigeria and much of Africa have walked this road with supranationals, who paint an interest in alleviating poverty in the so-called Third World.

During the 1960s, the World Bank financed FAO's plan of building dams on Ethiopia's Awash River Valley to make way for plantations growing sugar cane, cotton, and bananas However, the project produced a disaster for Ethiopians. The plan caused the removal of 20,000 residents and made Ethiopia accumulate a debt of $40 billion. Patricia Adams explains in "The World Bank and the IMF in Sub-Saharan Africa: Undermining

Development and Environmental Sustainability" that 42,000 Nigerians were evicted to allow construction of the Kainji dam, 12,600 evicted for the Ruzizi II dam in Zaire (Congo), and 80,000 removed in Ghana for the Akosombo dam. The Akosombo dam gave way to the largest human-made lake in the world, which caused the spread of the bilharzia disease for those who decided not to migrate. These sub-Saharan catastrophes are as accidental as the billions of animals that are slaughtered annually worldwide. There are no accidents in imperialism; these civilian casualties are merely itemized collateral damage, not happenstance.[29]

The major significance of Nigeria and Ghana's governments submitting to the wishes of US corporations and the WTO is a catastrophe for Africa at large, as both nations represent leadership for the Sub-Saharan area. Joining Egypt, South Africa, and Burkina Faso in cultivating GMO crops, soon other previously staunch opponents of GMO seeds will be dropping their bans as well. These efforts only mirror former colonial relationship tactics. Professor Agyeman Badu Akosa has been informing Africa that by systematically controlling Africa's food, the U.S. will have the opportunity to control its other investments on the continent.[30]

Nigerian architect and environmentalist Nnimmo Bassey, referring to his government's ill-conceived development, said in disgust: "You know how bad things have gone when public officials become Monsanto's spokespersons. The thrust of the industry is monopoly and profit."[31]

Latin America: Farmers in Brazil Fight Back

As US soybean exports to China have decreased substantially in 2015, Argentina hit record soybean stock levels, beating out every nation on the planet.[32] This development is not too surprising, since China has increased imports from Latin America during the 2000s, namely Argentina, Brazil, Chile, and Peru.[33] It had been a long time coming. Argentina is one of the earliest producers of GMOs. Not only is Argentina the third highest producer in GMO soybeans, it is also the largest exporter of soybean oil and derivatives.[34] During the takeoff of commercial US biotechnology in genetic engineering, Argentina did not hesitate to jump into the global market. It provided the push to usher GMO operations into Brazil and Mexico. Argentina increased Monsanto's profits from $60 million to $120 million between 2011 and 2015.[35]

A Mexico judge recently put a halt to genetically modified corn permits pending the results of the environmental lawsuits.[36] Because corn was first domesticated in Mexico, it creates for them a profound cultural significance in the battle between worker community and biotech operations.[37] There are three million farmers growing numerous varieties of corn. This makes Mexico exceptionally vital to biotech companies as a GMO seed producer. However, the injunction against GMO corn does not apply to other GMO crops. Other GMO crops may apply to be grown in Mexico.[38]

The Brazilian government dropped their ban of GMO crops in 2003 and quickly became the number two grower of maize and soybeans, behind the U.S.[39] As of March 2015, the second producer of soybean is Brazil, with 94,500 metric tonnes, 12,000 fewer than the U.S.[40] However, Brazil has not limited itself to just major crops of soybeans, maize, and cotton. This has caused a major upheaval among workers and farmers.

In 2015, the same year Brazil and Argentina saw a massive population in China ready to increase its Latin American GMO imports, 300 peasants of La Via Campesina organized a shutdown of the meeting of CTNBio in Brasilia.[41] In conjunction with the shutdown, there were roughly 1,000 women from the Landless Worker's Movement (MST) literally striking a blow to genetically modified organisms in São Paulo, Brazil.[42] The women, armed with sticks and knives, marched into a building in Itapetininga city, where biotech firm FutureGene Brazil Technology was based. MST did not harm anyone, but it managed to do significant damage to foil plans of the biotech industry, releasing GMO eucalyptus saplings. In a released statement, MST said the eucalyptus saplings contained a carcinogenic pesticide.

"When the pollen of the GM eucalyptus has the gene artificially inserted, any honey produced in the hives whose bees visit GM eucalyptus flowers will be contaminated by genetically modified material,"[43] said MST. Additionally, the women activists pointed out the large amount of pesticides, namely sulfuramid, which is described as a carcinogen and prohibited in 152 countries. Brazil's organization responsible for evaluating the safety of biotechnological products, National Technical Committee for Biosecurity (CTNBio), was due to approve the new GM product, but millions of plant samples were destroyed.

FutureGene Chief of Operations Eduardo Jose de Melo claimed "the product is safe for society and the environment. The losses were considerable, and we've lost multiple years of technological development." A month later in Brasilia, the CTNBio approved GMO eucalyptus trees.[44] The World Rainforest Movement International Coordinator Winnie Overbeek stated: "CTNBio has made many decisions in favor of releasing GMO crops in Brazil, ignoring protests and valid concerns from a wide range of groups of society. They also ignored protest letters signed by more than 100,000 people… The Commission systematically disregards the precautionary principle."[45] The battle on the ground to create a GMO-free Brazil is ever pressing.

12
CHINA DEVELOPS THE NON-GMO MARKET

China, the largest producer and importer of non-GMO soy, purchased this fall a record 13.18 million tons of GMO soybeans from the United States for the price of $5.3 billion, illustrating it is still in high demand of livestock feed.[1] Those numbers show a 55 percent lack in import sales in comparison to last year's US import numbers, and the U.S. is concerned. China is both strengthening its growing power around soybeans in attempts to accommodate its own nation's appetite for soybeans and manipulates the production of US soybean exports.[2] As the number one importer of soybeans worldwide, China has the power to fluctuate soybean stock and other stocks due to the numerous industries reliant on soybean products.

This combination is suspected to be less than accidental to the US government and business community. First, market manipulation was obvious when China's central bank devalued its currency by 2 percent, which has been a problem for the U.S. and the West for some time.[3] In one example, China having the largest nation with the greatest appetite for all commodities could be seen as breaking with US soy products. The devaluation of their yuan renminbi could also mean Chinese importers cannot purchase foreign products, only domestic. However, because the yuan is so low, Chinese exporters can move liberally throughout the market, making its own business sales globally.

If China suddenly limits its imports of US soybean, US farmers who have for years relied on China's massive soy hunger for most of its export can be negatively impacted. US farmers will be drowning in GMO crops they cannot unload. China, which occasionally stockpiles its soybeans, hit record import sales between 2013 and October, trading with Argentina and Brazil. This has helped Argentina and Brazil narrow the gap with the United States in GMO soybean production.

As for China empowering itself by developing its own national economy, partially through non-GMO soybean production, that is a long road. Nonetheless, China is adamant and proud of leading the distribution of non-GMO soybeans. The Chinese government has separated the trading between GMO and non-GMO soybeans and offered its farmers a higher purchase price for non-GMO producers, in addition to marketing assistance. China long recognized that much of the world perceives non-GMO soy as healthier. While morally apprehensible, the fact that China feeds its residents primarily non-GMO soybeans and its livestock animals all GMO soy from the U.S. is revealing.[4] However, data shows it will be years, if not a decade, before China can both meet its own non-GMO soybean demand and supply the world. US production in soybean is almost 10 times that of China.

Conclusion and Solution

This is not about your bag of GMO potato chips, although you can make your own potato chips in under 30 minutes. It is more about not being beholden to purchase a bag of some brand because you feel they have mastered potatoes. But where is the extremism in trying to make potato chips, your own sugar, eating less salt, or refraining from eating meat? I'm not recommending cutting back on meat, I'm suggesting a systematic change in our global food.

My mission in writing this was to craft a text that outlined an easier path towards veganism. I set out to help most of the world find easier ways to eat vegan. Some places may substitute peas for mung beans, or spinach for cassava leaves. I hope that is the case. As the only sensible alternative, I also want to address veganism as it intersects with agriculture, capitalism, and globalism.

Veganism in the United States is marketed in such a way to appeal to the consumer who purchases genetically engineered foods, not because they think they are safe, but generally because they may not know. We are unaware of the consequences of consumption and apathetic to its effects on the so-called Third World. In simple terms, we see things advertised as answers to our imperfections, and we want those things regardless of the cost to us and others.

There are solutions.

The global food system conundrum facing new and longstanding vegans is not without solutions. However, veganism is definitely part of the equation. The old way is not sustainable for our bodies and planet. The first step is to learn and evaluate the useful tips on how to go vegan. Eliminate cancer and diseased meats, no matter how "humanely" they are marketed. That marketing term does not make sense to the animal.

Hopefully you have transitioned into a vegan or semi-vegan lifestyle. Examine for yourself whether soy works for you. Frankenstein's monster was once a man. Soybeans are still just beans. I encourage you to find products made with organically grown, non-GMO soybeans.

The problem with selecting GMO products is not just a potential health risk, which has proven true in the case of rBGH and cancers, but also its impact on humanity and animals around the world. For animals, it leaves them vulnerable to injections and other biotechnological creations. It places a strain on animals who have to work harder to keep up with the artificial increases in food production before they are slaughtered.

For so-called Third-World farming communities, competing within the global market with their non-GMO products places them at the mercy of GMO farmers, because they do not have the marketing power to be heard. Choosing GMO also forces developing farmers to go GMO, and that's not a good idea either, because it makes options for everyone else less available. This is not merely the ventures of capitalism failing low-income people of color; this is the global elite utilizing capitalism to fail those struggling to develop after having been subject to oppressive forces during periods of colonial rule. Globalism is just privatized colonization.

In reality, whether there are GMO crops or not, under globalism exists imperialism. Even in a world of no genetically modified organisms, transnationals like FAO and WTO work at the behest of the United States and other Western nations. Their businessmen and politicians collaborate to hold on to the world's resources to sustain imperialism and, of course, to get a piece of the pie for themselves. Under capitalism, if your productivity is 0.5 percent less in March of 2016 than it was in March of 2015, you can be terminated in the United States. That is capitalism. But if you're in the "Third World" under a government contract with FAO to grow crops at a higher rate to offset debt with the IMF or World Bank, you will be expected to work forever as a serf on your own land. Like so many thousands of farmers in India, you resort to committing suicide. Cheryl Payer stated: "The IMF has been the chosen instrument for imposing imperialist financial discipline upon poor countries under a facade of multilateralism and technical competence."[1] In short, the European Union and the Western nations, or simply white-led nations, may be able to ignore supranationals, but the nations forced to pay will always be those that have been formerly colonized, impoverished, and Black or Brown.

The way in which the ordinary consumer can help reduce pain and animal cruelty is first by going vegan. That will increase chances of living and learning more about the only world you and your family and friends inhabit. Know what you're buying in the supermarket. What you do not know about a product can potentially harm you and your loved ones or have disastrous effects on other beings and your planet. If you like a potential product and wish to continue consuming it, read the label and find out what it's made of and its place of origin. Companies generally leave their address and phone number to contact them.

For the many institutions interested in creating a world that is habitable for the next 100 years, invest in people, animals, and plants and make your decision. While the idea of understanding imperialism and becoming vegan might seem difficult to grasp, remember that it was only in 1976 that the first biotech company, Genentech, was founded in the United States.[2] By 1996, foods made in a lab were in your supermarket. Those foods are, at the most basic level, farming and agriculture crops. We can plant those same foods and we can decide not to choose GMO with the rest of the world. I can't emphasize enough that we live in the only nation that will not properly label our food.

With the internet sophistication of disseminating new information about heart disease and cancers, and the World Health Organization (WHO) addressing processed meat (which is most meat you'll eat) being cancerous, the new resurgence of vegetarianism, and especially veganism, happened in the mainstream, and the system is adapting to you and the unknown.[3] Already integrated is a system of genetically engineered foods targeting all crops, because you just might go in that direction. And since you might stay in the past, know that pigs are being tested for GMOs too, because you love bacon. The margin for error will be greater with more complex organisms. In 2002, Dr. Malcolm Devine, the head scientist at Aventis CropScience, said: "there's a 60–70% chance that your products in the supermarket are GMO."[4] That's 20 years ago.

The reason why labeling didn't work in the U.S. is because it would have affected most of your favorite products. That labeling change would have cost billions. Not to mention that the fear of GMO products would have forced consumers to purchase products overseas, probably bankrupting hundreds, if not thousands, of businesses. The US government and businesses thought that your health is not that important. But it's a venture with profits, not your life. Nothing is new about globalism, except for GMOs. It's been vicious and dependent, and especially parasitic to workers and people of color around the world.

The public has to become less apathetic to suffering—it's that simple. Bring in someone to discuss globalism and veganism. Learn how to grow your own food and prepare it. Understand how to interpret emerging policies. Find out where your allies are.

The industry has made up its mind with regards to your health and the health of the planet. The next move is ours. Are we going to align with the rest of the farmers and workers of the world, or continue on as if they don't exist and we don't know any better? The U.S. has better access to resources today. Wherever we are resourceful, we need to employ those talents to work for us. Be local and global.

ENDNOTES

Introduction

1. Peet, Richard. (2009). *Unholy Trinity: The IMF, World Bank and WTO*. (2nd Edition) (New York: Zed).

Food Soverignty Under the Unapologetically Black Framework

1. Passy, Jacob (2022). "The Gap in Credit Access Is Growing Along Racial Lines": Black Applicants Are Denied a Mortgage 84% More Often than White Peers. MarketWatch, January 17, https://www.marketwatch.com/story/the-gap-in-credit-access-is-growing-black-applicants-are-denied-a-mortgage-84-more-often-than-white-peers-11642099864.

2. Duster, Chandelis & Boschma, Janie (2021). Many Black Farmers Nationwide Struggling to Keep Their Farms Afloat as They Face Disparities Across the Board. *CNN Politics*, December 15, https://www.cnn.com/2021/12/15/politics/black-farmers-debt-relief-disparities/index.html.

3. USDA National Agricultural Statistics Service (2020). Census of Agriculture: 2017 Race, Ethnicity and Gender Profiles, September 2, https://www.nass.usda.gov/Publications/AgCensus/2017/Online_Resources/Race,_Ethnicity_and_Gender_Profiles/.

1. Heart Disease, Obesity, and Fast Food

1. Youth Bible Speaks Community SDA Church. Touch of Health – Dr. Milton Mills 12/3/2020, https://www.youtube.com/watch?v=OsYe-dPjq2E.

2. Centers for Disease Control and Prevention (2007). Prevalence of Heart Disease—United States, 2005, February 16, https://www.cdc.gov/mmwr/preview/mmwrhtml/mm5606a2.htm.

3. Centers for Disease Control and Prevention (2022). Heart Disease Facts, February 7, https://www.cdc.gov/heartdisease/facts.htm.

4. Ibid.

5. Ibid.

6. Ibid.

7. Centers for Disease Control and Prevention (2022). Heart Disease, January 28, https://www.cdc.gov/heartdisease/.

8. Centers for Disease Control and Prevention (2022). Heart Disease Facts, February 7, https://www.cdc.gov/heartdisease/facts.htm.

9. Centers for Disease Control and Prevention (2022). Overweight & Obesity, February 17, https://www.cdc.gov/obesity/index.html.

10. Centers for Disease Control and Prevention (2022). Adult Obesity Facts, May 17, https://www.cdc.gov/obesity/data/adult.html.

11. Ibid.

12. Centers for Disease Control and Prevention (2022). Overweight & Obesity, February 17, https://www.cdc.gov/obesity/index.html.

13. Ibid.

14. Toro, Ross (2012). Leading Causes of Death in the US: 1990–Present (Infographic). *LiveScience*, July 1, https://www.livescience.com/21213-leading-causes-of-death-in-the-u-s-since-1900-infographic.html.

15. Ibid.

16. Watson, Alan (2012). Illustrated History of Heart Disease 1825–2015: The Twists and Turns of Absurd Dietary Advice. *Diet Heart News*, August 19, https://www.sott.net/article/292552-Illustrated-history-of-heart-disease-1825-2015-The-twists-and-turns-of-absurd-dietary-advice.

17. Watson, Alan (2012). Illustrated History of Heart Disease 1825–2015: The Twists and Turns of Absurd Dietary Advice. *Diet Heart News*, August 19, https://www.sott.net/article/292552-Illustrated-history-of-heart-disease-1825-2015-The-twists-and-turns-of-absurd-dietary-advice.

18. Truswell, A. Stewart & Darnton-Hill, Ian (1981). Food Habits of Adolescents. *Nutrition Reviews* 39(2): 73-88, https://doi.org/10.1111/j.1753-4887.1981.tb06736.x.

19. Ibid.

20. Ibid.

21. Ibid.

22. Ibid.

23. Ibid.

24. McSpotlight (n.d.). A Brief History of McDonald's, https://www.mcspotlight.org/company/company_history.html.

25. Sherwood, Nancy E., Story, Mary, Neumark-Sztainer, et al. (2001). Behavioral Risk Factors for Obesity: Diet and Physical Activity. In Coulston, Ann M., Rock, Cheryl L., & Monsen, Elaine R. (eds.), *Nutrition in the Prevention and Treatment of Disease* (1st Edition) (Cambridge: Academic Press).

26. Ibid.

27. Centers for Disease Control and Prevention (2022). National Health and Nutrition Examination Survey, May 6, https://www.cdc.gov/nchs/nhanes/index.htm.

28. Truswell, A. Stewart & Darnton-Hill, Ian (1981). Food Habits of Adolescents. *Nutrition Reviews* 39(2): 73-88, https://doi.org/10.1111/j.1753-4887.1981.tb06736.x.

29. Sherwood, Nancy E., Story, Mary, Neumark-Sztainer, et al. (2001). Behavioral Risk Factors for Obesity: Diet and Physical Activity. In Coulston, Ann M., Rock, Cheryl L., & Monsen, Elaine R. (eds.), *Nutrition in the Prevention and Treatment of Disease* (1st Edition) (Cambridge: Academic Press).

30. McSpotlight (n.d.). A Brief History of McDonald's, https://www.mcspotlight.org/company/company_history.html.

31. Ibid.

32. Ibid.

33. McDonald's Corporation (2014). McDonald's Corporation 2014 Annual Report, https://corporate.mcdonalds.com/content/dam/gwscorp/nfl/investor-relations-content/annual-reports/McDonalds2014AnnualReport.PDF.

34. U.S. Department of Agriculture (2015). FY 2015 Budget Summary and Annual Performance Plan, https://www.usda.gov/sites/default/files/documents/fy15-budget-summary.pdf.

35. Sherwood, Nancy E., Story, Mary, Neumark-Sztainer, et al. (2001). Behavioral Risk Factors for Obesity: Diet and Physical Activity. In Coulston, Ann M., Rock, Cheryl L., & Monsen, Elaine R. (eds.), *Nutrition in the Prevention and Treatment of Disease* (1st Edition) (Cambridge: Academic Press).

36. Fryar, Cheryl D., & Ervin, R. Bethene (2013). Caloric Intake from Fast Food Among Adults: United States, 2007–2010. *NCHS Data Brief* (114), https://www.cdc.gov/nchs/data/databriefs/db114.pdf.

37. Let's Move: America's Move to Raise a Healthier Generation of Kids (2017). Let's Move Blog, https://letsmove.obamawhitehouse.archives.gov/.

38. Ibid.

3. Vitamin B-12

1. Shreeram, Sathyavageeswaran, Johns, Paul W., Subramaniam, Swaminathan, et al. (2014). The Relative Bioavailability of the Calcium Salt of β-Hydroxy-β-Methylbutyrate Is Greater than That of the Free Fatty Acid Form in Rats. *Journal of Nutrition* 144(10): 1549–1555, https://doi.org/10.3945/jn.114.196527.

4. Vegan Proteins

1. Bussone, Danielle (2015). How Do I get Adequate Protein? In Bussone, Danielle, *Time for Change: Whole Foods for Whole Health!* (Abingdon, VA: Danrich Publishing).

2. Shimomura, Yoshiharu, Murakami, Taro, Nakai, Naoya, et al. (2004). Exercise Promotes BCAA Catabolism: Effects of BCAA Supplementation on Skeletal Muscle During Exercise. *The Journal of Nutrition* 134(6): 1583S–1587S, https://doi.org/10.1093/jn/134.6.1583S.

5. Seitan

1. Wikipedia (2022). Seitan, May 20, https://en.wikipedia.org/wiki/Seitan.

2. Bob's Red Mill (2022). Vital Wheat Gluten Flour, https://www.bobsredmill.com/vital-wheat-gluten.html.

3. Ibid.

4.   Celiac Disease Foundation (n.d.). What Is Celiac Disease?, https://celiac.org/about-celiac-disease/what-is-celiac-disease/.

7. Understanding Wild Hybrids

1.   C., J. M. (1914). Anatomy and Plant Hybrids. *Botanical Gazette* 57(4): 341, https://doi.org/10.1086/331312.

2.   Crystal, Philip A., & Jacobs, Douglass F. (2014). Drought and Flood Stress Tolerance of Butternut (*Juglans Cinerea*) and Naturally Occurring Hybrids: Implications for Restoration. *Canadian Journal of Forest Research* 44(10): 1206–1216, https://doi.org/10.1139/cjfr-2014-0151.

3   Mirimin, L., Kerwath, S.E., Macey, B.M., et al. (2014). Identification of Naturally Occurring Hybrids Between Two Overexploited Sciaenid Species Along the South African Coast. *Molecular Phylogenetics and Evolution* 76: 30–33, https://doi.org/10.1016/j.ympev.2014.02.010.

4.   Focke, Wilhelm Obers (1913). History of Plant Hybrids. *The Monist* 23(3): 396–416, https://www.jstor.org/stable/27900440.

8. Phytoestrogens and Their Relationship to Humans and Animals

1.   Dixon, Richard A. (2004). Phytoestrogens. *Annual Review of Plant Biology* 55: 225–261, https://doi.org/10.1146/annurev.arplant.55.031903.141729.

2.   Chen, Meinan, Rao, Yanhua, Zheng, Yi, et al. (2014) Association Between Soy Isoflavone Intake and Breast Cancer Risk for Pre- and Post-Menopausal Women: A Meta-Analysis of Epidemiological Studies. *PLoS ONE* 9(2): e89288, https://doi.org/10.1371/journal.pone.0089288.

3.   Rickard, Sharon E., & Thompson, Lilian U. (1997). Phytoestrogens and Lignans: Effects on Reproduction and Chronic Disease. *ACS Symposium Series* 662: 273–293, https://doi.org/10.1021/bk-1997-0662.ch016.

4.   Linus Pauling Institute, Micronutrient Information Center (n.d.). Lignans. Oregon State University, https://lpi.oregonstate.edu/mic/dietary-factors/phytochemicals/lignans.

5. Rickard, Sharon E., & Thompson, Lilian U. (1997). Phytoestrogens and Lignans: Effects on Reproduction and Chronic Disease. *ACS Symposium Series* 662: 273–293, https://doi.org/10.1021/bk-1997-0662.ch016.

6. Ibid.

7. Conroy, Shannon M., Maskarinec, Gertraud, Park, Song-Yi, et al. (2013) The Effects of Soy Consumption Before Diagnosis on Breast Cancer Survival: The Multiethnic Cohort Study. *Nutrition and Cancer 65(4): 527–537,* https://doi.org/10.1080/01635581.2013.776694.

8. Wasserman, Michael D., Milton, Katharine, & Chapman, Colin A. (2013). The Roles of Phytoestrogens in Primate Ecology and Evolution. *International Journal of Primatology 34(5): 861–878, https://doi.org/*10.1080/01635581.2013.776694.

9. Ibid.

10. Ibid.

11. Ibid.

12. The Weston A. Price Foundation (n.d.). Soy Alert!, https://www.westonaprice.org/soy-alert/.

13. Wasserman, Michael D., Milton, Katharine, & Chapman, Colin A. (2013). The Roles of Phytoestrogens in Primate Ecology and Evolution. *International Journal of Primatology* 34(5): 861–878, https://doi.org/10.1080/01635581.2013.776694.

14. De Meester, Fabien, Zibadi, Sherma, & Watson, Ronald Ross (eds.) (2010). *Modern Dietary Fat Intakes in Disease Promotion* (Totowa, NJ: Humana Press).

15. Mense, Sarah M., Hei, Tom K., Ganju, Ramesh K., et al. (2008). Phytoestrogens and Breast Cancer Prevention: Possible Mechanisms of Action. *Environmental Heath Perspectives* 116(4): 426–433, https://doi.org/10.1289/ehp.10538.

16. Linus Pauling Institute, Micronutrient Information Center (n.d.). Lignans. Oregon State University, https://lpi.oregonstate.edu/mic/dietary-factors/phytochemicals/lignans.

17. Chen, Meinan, Rao, Yanhua, Zheng, Yi, et al. (2014) Association Between Soy Isoflavone Intake and Breast Cancer Risk for Pre- and

Post-Menopausal Women: A Meta-Analysis of Epidemiological Studies. *PLoS ONE* 9(2): e89288, https://doi.org/10.1371/journal.pone.0089288.

18. Ibid.

19. Conroy, Shannon M., Maskarinec, Gertraud, Park, Song-Yi, et al. (2013) The Effects of Soy Consumption Before Diagnosis on Breast Cancer Survival: The Multiethnic Cohort Study. *Nutrition and Cancer* 65(4): 527–537, https://doi.org/10.1080/01635581.2013.776694.

20. Fritz, Heidi, Seely, Dugald, Flower, Gillian, et al. (2013). Soy, Red Clover, and Isoflavones and Breast Cancer: A Systematic Review. *PLoS ONE* 8(11): e81968, https://doi.org/10.1371/journal.pone.0081968.

21. Wu, Ying-Chao, Zheng, Dong, Sun, Jin-Jie, et al. (2015). Meta-Analysis of Studies on Breast Cancer Risk and Diet in Chinese Women. *International Journal of Clinical and Experimental Medicine* 8(1):73–85, https://www.ncbi.nlm.nih.gov/pmc/articles/PMC4358431/.

22. Mense, Sarah M., Hei, Tom K., Ganju, Ramesh K., et al. (2008). Phytoestrogens and Breast Cancer Prevention: Possible Mechanisms of Action. *Environmental Heath Perspectives* 116(4): 426–433, https://doi.org/10.1289/ehp.10538.

23. Fritz, Heidi, Seely, Dugald, Flower, Gillian, et al. (2013). Soy, Red Clover, and Isoflavones and Breast Cancer: A Systematic Review. *PLoS ONE* 8(11): e81968, https://doi.org/10.1371/journal.pone.0081968.

24. Ibid.

25. Ibid.

26. Conroy, Shannon M., Maskarinec, Gertraud, Park, Song-Yi, et al. (2013) The Effects of Soy Consumption Before Diagnosis on Breast Cancer Survival: The Multiethnic Cohort Study. *Nutrition and Cancer* 65(4): 527–537, https://doi.org/10.1080/01635581.2013.776694.

27. Rickard, Sharon E., & Thompson, Lilian U. (1997). Phytoestrogens and Lignans: Effects on Reproduction and Chronic Disease. *ACS*

    Symposium Series 662: 273–293, https://doi.org/10.1021/bk-1997-0662.ch016.

28. Linus Pauling Institute, Micronutrient Information Center (n.d.). Lignans. Oregon State University, https://lpi.oregonstate.edu/mic/dietary-factors/phytochemicals/lignans.

29. Durazzo, Alessandra, Azzini, Elena, Turfani, Valeria, et al. (2013). Effects of Cooking on Lignans Content in Whole-Grain Pasta Made with Different Cereals and Other Seeds. *Cereal Chemistry Journal* 90(2): 169–171, https://doi.org/10.1094/CCHEM-05-12-0065-N.

30. Linus Pauling Institute, Micronutrient Information Center (n.d.). Lignans. Oregon State University, https://lpi.oregonstate.edu/mic/dietary-factors/phytochemicals/lignans.

31. Ibid.

31. Mense, Sarah M., Hei, Tom K., Ganju, Ramesh K., et al. (2008). Phytoestrogens and Breast Cancer Prevention: Possible Mechanisms of Action. *Environmental Heath Perspectives* 116(4): 426–433, https://doi.org/10.1289/ehp.10538.

33. Ibid.

34. Houck, James P. (1964). A Statistical Model of the Demand for Soybeans. *Journal of Farm Economics* 46(2): 366–374, https://doi.org/10.2307/1236541.

35. Kerr, Gord (2019). Soy Protein Vs. Meat Protein. Livestrong.com, February 21, https://www.livestrong.com/article/240951-soy-protein-vs-meat-protein/.

36. Messina, Mark (2014). Soy Foods, Isoflavones, and the Health of Postmenopausal Women. *American Journal of Clinical Nutrition* 100: 423–430, https://doi.org/10.3945/ajcn.113.071464.

37. Eating China: Chinese Food History, Culture and Recipes (n.d.) Soy Story: The History of the Soybean, https://www.eatingchina.com/articles/soystory.htm.

38. Mote, Frederick W. (2003) China and the World in Early Qing Times. In Mote, Frederick W., *Imperial China, 900–1800* (Cambridge: Harvard University Press).

39. Houck, James P. (1964). A Statistical Model of the Demand for Soybeans. *Journal of Farm Economics* 46(2): 366–374, https://doi.org/10.2307/1236541.

40. Ibid.

41. Messina, Mark (2014). Soy Foods, Isoflavones, and the Health of Postmenopausal Women. *American Journal of Clinical Nutrition* 100: 423–430, https://doi.org/10.3945/ajcn.113.071464.

9. The Rise of U.S. Genetically Modified Organisms (GMOs)

1. Eating China: Chinese Food History, Culture and Recipes (n.d.) Soy Story: The History of the Soybean, https://www.eatingchina.com/articles/soystory.htm.

2. Shoemaker, Robbin, Harwood, Joy, Rubenstein, Kelly Day, et al. (2001). Economic Issues in Agricultural Biotechnology. USDA Economic Research Service, March 19, https://www.ers.usda.gov/publications/pub-details/?pubid=42313.

3. Ibid.

4. Price, Becky, & Cotter, Janet (2014). The GM Contamination Register: A Review of Recorded Contamination Incidents Associated with Genetically Modified Organisms (GMOs), 1997–2013. *International Journal of Food Contamination* 1(5), https://doi.org/10.1186/s40550-014-0005-8.

5. Shoemaker, Robbin, Harwood, Joy, Rubenstein, Kelly Day, et al. (2001). Economic Issues in Agricultural Biotechnology. USDA Economic Research Service, March 19, https://www.ers.usda.gov/publications/pub-details/?pubid=42313.

6. Fernandez-Cornejo, Jorge, Wechsler, Seth, Livingston, Mike, et al. (2014). Genetically Engineered Crops in the United States. USDA-ERS Economic Research Report (162), http://dx.doi.org/10.2139/ssrn.2503388.

7. Ibid.

8. Ibid.

9. Ibid.

10. Ibid.

11. Ibid.

12. Ibid.

13. Ibid.

14. Ibid.

15. Ibid.

16. Price, Becky, & Cotter, Janet (2014). The GM Contamination Register: A Review of Recorded Contamination Incidents Associated with Genetically Modified Organisms (GMOs), 1997–2013. *International Journal of Food Contamination* 1(5), https://doi.org/10.1186/s40550-014-0005-8.

17. Noor, Jaisal (2013). New GMO Crops Temporarily Blocked in Mexico. *The Real News*, November 2, https://www.dailykos.com/stories/2013/11/2/1252551/-New-GMO-Crops-Temporarily-Blocked-in-Mexico.

18. Fernandez-Cornejo, Jorge, Wechsler, Seth, Livingston, Mike, et al. (2014). Genetically Engineered Crops in the United States. USDA-ERS Economic Research Report (162), http://dx.doi.org/10.2139/ssrn.2503388.

19. Ibid.

20. Ibid.

21. Ibid.

22. Ibid.

23. Code of Federal Regulations (2012). Title 21: Food and Drugs, April 1, https://www.govinfo.gov/content/pkg/CFR-2012-title21-vol3/pdf/CFR-2012-title21-vol3.pdf.

24. Supermarket Guru (2011). Consumers' Soy Habits, November 21, https://www.supermarketguru.com/articles/consumers-soy-habits/.

25. USDA National Agricultural Statistics Service (n.d.). 2013/2014 Export Report, https://www.nass.usda.gov/.

26. Houck, James P. (1964). A Statistical Model of the Demand for Soybeans. *Journal of Farm Economics* 46(2): 366–374, https://doi.org/10.2307/1236541.

27. "2013/2014 Export Report." Hyperlink illegible in the PDF. United States, 2015. Web. 6 Nov. 2015.

28. Ibid.

29. Ibid.

30. Zheng, Shi, & Wang, Zhigang (2013). Pricing Efficiency in the Chinese NGM and GM Soybean Futures Market. *China: An International Journal* 11(3): 48–67, https://go.gale.com/ps/i.do?id=-GALE%7CA354661783&sid=googleScholar&v=2.1&it=r&link-access=abs&issn=02197472&p=AONE&sw=w&userGroupName=-nysl_oweb.

10. The European Union: An Informed Public

1. Pollack, Mark A., & Shaffer, Gregory C. (2000). Biotechnology: The Next Transatlantic Trade War? *The Washington Quarterly* 23(4): 41–54, https://doi.org/10.1162/016366000561330.

2. Shoemaker, Robbin, Harwood, Joy, Rubenstein, Kelly Day, et al. (2001). Economic Issues in Agricultural Biotechnology. USDA Economic Research Service, March 19, https://www.ers.usda.gov/publications/pub-details/?pubid=42313.

3. Pollack, Mark A., & Shaffer, Gregory C. (2000). Biotechnology: The Next Transatlantic Trade War? *The Washington Quarterly* 23(4): 41–54, https://doi.org/10.1162/016366000561330.

4. Anderson, Molly D. (2013). The Role of US Consumers and Producers in Food Sovereignty. Food Sovereignty: A Critical Dialogue, https://www.tni.org/files/download/31_anderson_2013.pdf.

5. Holstead, Joseph. (2007). Recombinant Bovine Growth Hormone. *Connecticut General Assembly.* https://www.cga.ct.gov/2007/rpt/2007-R-0159.htm.

6. James, Sallie. "Food Safety Policy in the WTO Era." In The Economics of Quarantine and the SPS Agreement, edited by Kym Anderson, Cheryl McRae, and David Wilson, 332–52. University of Adelaide Press, 2001. http://www.jstor.org/stable/10.20851/j.ctt1t304rx.23.

7. GMO-Free Regions (n.d.). GMO Cultivation Bans in Europe, https://www.gmo-free-regions.org/gmo-free-regions/bans.html.

8. Price, Becky, & Cotter, Janet (2014). The GM Contamination Register: A Review of Recorded Contamination Incidents Associated with Genetically Modified Organisms (GMOs), 1997–

2013. *International Journal of Food Contamination* 1(5), https://doi.org/10.1186/s40550-014-0005-8.

9. Anderson, Molly D. (2013). The Role of US Consumers and Producers in Food Sovereignty. Food Sovereignty: A Critical Dialogue, https://www.tni.org/files/download/31_anderson_2013.pdf.

10. Reuters (2015). Syngenta Withdraws Two EU Applications for GMO Products, October 13, https://www.reuters.com/article/syngenta-gmo/syngenta-withdraws-two-eu-applications-for-gmo-products-idUSL8N12D4AD20151013.

11. Ibid.

12. The Greens/EFA in the European Parliament (2015). EU Parliament Rejects Flawed GMO Food and Feed Opt-Outs Proposal, October 28, https://www.greens-efa.eu/en/article/press/gmo-authorisation-6170.

13. Rhodes-Vivour, Gbadebo (2015). Federal Agencies as Unwitting Pawns in Re-Colonisation (1). *The Guardian*, August 31, https://guardian.ng/opinion/federal-agencies-as-unwitting-pawns-in-re-colonisation-1/.

14. Center for Science in the Public Interest (1999). Statement of Michael F. Jacobson, Ph.D., Executive Director, Center for Science in the Public Interest to the Food and Drug Administration, November 18, https://www.cspinet.org/new/genetics_fda.html.

15. Greenpeace European Unit (2016). Greenpeace: Time to Hit the Stop Button on TTIP, July 15, https://www.greenpeace.org/eu-unit/issues/democracy-europe/626/greenpeace-time-to-hit-the-stop-button-on-ttip/.

16. Shoemaker, Robbin, Harwood, Joy, Rubenstein, Kelly Day, et al. (2001). Economic Issues in Agricultural Biotechnology. USDA Economic Research Service, March 19, https://www.ers.usda.gov/publications/pub-details/?pubid=42313.

11. The Third World: A Worldview of Agricultural Trade

1. Peschard, Karine (2014). Farmers' Rights and Food Sovereignty: Critical Insights from India. *The Journal of Peasant Studies* 41(6): 1085–1108, https://doi.org/10.1080/03066150.2014.937338.

2. World Trade Organization (1994). Agreement on Trade-Related

Aspects of Intellectual Property Rights (Unamended), https://www.wto.org/english/docs_e/legal_e/27-trips_01_e.htm.

3. Peschard, Karine (2014). Farmers' Rights and Food Sovereignty: Critical Insights from India. *The Journal of Peasant Studies* 41(6): 1085–1108, https://doi.org/10.1080/03066150.2014.937338.

4. Ibid.

5. World Trade Organization (1994). Agreement on Trade-Related Aspects of Intellectual Property Rights (Unamended), https://www.wto.org/english/docs_e/legal_e/27-trips_01_e.htm.

6. Price, Becky, & Cotter, Janet (2014). The GM Contamination Register: A Review of Recorded Contamination Incidents Associated with Genetically Modified Organisms (GMOs), 1997–2013. *International Journal of Food Contamination* 1(5), https://doi.org/10.1186/s40550-014-0005-8.

7. Shiva, Vandana (n.d.). Seed Freedom and Food Democracy. Navdanya International, https://navdanyainternational.org/cause/seed-freedom-and-food-democracy/.

8. Ibid.

9. Seed Freedom (2014). Dr. Vandana Shiva Visits Sri Lanka, July 7, https://www.youtube.com/watch?v=b-jhAuGF8pE.

10. Ibid.

11. Bishop, John (dir.) (2002). *Deconstructing Supper* (Bullfrog Films).

12. Express Web Desk (2021). Farmers End Year-Long Protest: A Timeline of How It Unfolded. *The Indian Express*, December 9, https://indianexpress.com/article/india/one-year-of-farm-laws-timeline-7511961/.

13. Shiva, Vandana (n.d.). Seed Freedom and Food Democracy. Navdanya International, https://navdanyainternational.org/cause/seed-freedom-and-food-democracy/.

14. Kurukulasuriya, Lasanda (2014). Sri Lankan Farmers Resist New Seed Law. *New Internationalist*, January 28, https://newint.org/blog/majority/2014/01/28/sri-lanka-seed-law.

15. Ikhwan, Mohammed (2009). Asian Peoples' Movement Against ADB. La Via Campesina, May 12, https://viacampesina.org/en/asian-peoples-movement-against-adb/.

16. Seed Freedom (2014). Dr. Vandana Shiva Visits Sri Lanka, July 7, https://www.youtube.com/watch?v=b-jhAuGF8pE.

17. Paarlberg, Robert (2010). GMO Foods and Crops: Africa's Choice. *New Biotechnology* 27(5): 609–613, https://doi.org/10.1016/j.nbt.2010.07.005.

18. Zerbe, Noah (2004). Feeding the Famine? American Food Aid and the GMO Debate in Southern Africa. *Food Policy* 29(6): 593–608, https://doi.org/10.1016/j.foodpol.2004.09.002.

19. Ibid.

20. Ibid.

21. Ibid.

22. Modern Ghana (2015). Biotechnology May Not Be a Panacea for Food Security, March 4, https://www.modernghana.com/news/602457/biotechnology-not-be-a-panacea-for-food-security.html.

23. Alliance for Food Sovereignty in Africa (2015). ARIPO Sells Out African Farmers, Seals Secret Deal on Plant Variety Protection. Association for Plant Breeding for the Benefit of Society, July 8, https://www.apbrebes.org/news/aripo-sells-out-african-farmers-seals-secret-deal-plant-variety-protection-%C2%A0.

24. Europa (2015). Court Dismisses Application Against Production of GMO Foods. Pulse, October 29, https://www.pulse.com.gh/ece-frontpage/judgement-court-dismisses-application-against-production-of-gmo-foods/nwbmskx.

25. Rhodes-Vivour, Gbadebo (2015). Federal Agencies as Unwitting Pawns in Re-Colonisation (1). *The Guardian*, August 31, https://guardian.ng/opinion/federal-agencies-as-unwitting-pawns-in-re-colonisation-1/.

26. Isaac, Nkechi (2015). Nigeria: President Signs Biosafety Bill into Law. All Africa, April 22, https://allafrica.com/stories/201504221000.html.

27. Ibid.

28. Bernstein, Henry (2014). Food Sovereignty via the "Peasant Way": A Skeptical View. *The Journal of Peasant Studies* 41(6): 1031–1063, https://doi.org/10.1080/03066150.2013.852082.

29. Adams, Patricia (1992). The World Bank and the IMF in Sub-Saharan Africa: Understanding Development and Environmental Sustainability. *Journal of International Affairs* 46(1): 97–117, https://www.jstor.org/stable/24384118.

30. Peace FM (2014). America Using GMOs to Control the World, March 7, https://www.peacefmonline.com/pages/local/news/201403/192186.php.

31. Rhodes-Vivour, Gbadebo (2015). Federal Agencies as Unwitting Pawns in Re-Colonisation (1). *The Guardian*, August 31, https://guardian.ng/opinion/federal-agencies-as-unwitting-pawns-in-re-colonisation-1/.

32. Vulcan, Tom (2015). Soybeans Outlook Relies on China's Ravenous Appetite. Seeking Alpha, April 28, https://seekingalpha.com/article/3108176-soybeans-outlook-relies-on-chinas-ravenous-appetite.

33. Ellis, Evan R (2009). *China in Latin America: The Whats and Wherefores* (Boulder, CO: Lynne Rienner).

34. Fernandez-Cornejo, Jorge, Wechsler, Seth, Livingston, Mike, et al. (2014). Genetically Engineered Crops in the United States. USDA-ERS Economic Research Report (162), http://dx.doi.org/10.2139/ssrn.2503388.

35. Bronstein, Hugh (2012). Interview-Monsanto bullish on Argentine corn, sees output jump. *Reuters*. https://www.reuters.com/article/argentina-monsanto-corn-idAFL2E8J1IE720120802.

36. Noor, Jaisal (2013). New GMO Crops Temporarily Blocked in Mexico. *The Real News*, November 2, https://www.dailykos.com/stories/2013/11/2/1252551/-New-GMO-Crops-Temporarily-Blocked-in-Mexico.

37. Ibid.

38. Price, Becky, & Cotter, Janet (2014). The GM Contamination Register: A Review of Recorded Contamination Incidents Associated with Genetically Modified Organisms (GMOs), 1997–2013. *International Journal of Food Contamination* 1(5), https://doi.org/10.1186/s40550-014-0005-8.

39. Ortiz, Fabíola (2013). A Decade of Legal GM Soy in Brazil. Inter Press Service, July 30, http://www.ipsnews.net/2013/07/a-decade-of-legal-gm-soy-in-brazil/.

40. Stronzake, Judite, & Wolford, Wendy (2016). Brazil's Landless Workers Rise Up. *Dissent Magazine*, https://www.dissentmagazine.org/article/brazils-landless-workers-rise-mst-land-occupation.

41. Vulcan, Tom (2015). Soybeans Outlook Relies on China's Ravenous Appetite. Seeking Alpha, April 28, https://seekingalpha.com/article/3108176-soybeans-outlook-relies-on-chinas-ravenous-appetite.

42. PR Newswire (2015). GMO Trees Approved in Brazil: Groups Denounce Illegal Decision, April 10, https://www.prnewswire.com/news-releases/gmo-trees-approved-in-brazil-groups-denounce-illegal-decision-300064002.html.

43. Stronzake, Judite, & Wolford, Wendy (2016). Brazil's Landless Workers Rise Up. *Dissent Magazine*, https://www.dissentmagazine.org/article/brazils-landless-workers-rise-mst-land-occupation.

44. The Campaign to Stop GE Trees (2015). Brazil Govt Approves GMO Eucalyptus Trees: Groups Denounce Illegal Decision, April 9, https://stopgetrees.org/brazil-govt-approves-gmo-eucalyptus-trees-groups-denounce-illegal-decision/.

45. Ibid.

12. China Developing the GMO Market

1. Zheng, Shi, & Wang, Zhigang (2013). Pricing Efficiency in the Chinese NGM and GM Soybean Futures Market. *China: An International Journal* 11(3): 48–67, https://go.gale.com/ps/i.do?id=GALE%7CA354661783&sid=googleScholar&v=2.1&it=r&linkaccess=abs&issn=02197472&p=AONE&sw=w&userGroupName=nysl_oweb.

2. Wilson, Jeff (2015). China Boosts Annual U.S. Soybean Purchase Accord to Record. *Bloomberg*, September 24, https://www.bloomberg.com/news/articles/2015-09-24/china-trade-delegation-to-buy-u-s-soybeans-worth-5-3-billion-ieyjdeu4.

3. Irwin, Neil (2015). Why Did China Devalue Its Currency? Two Big Reasons. *The New York Times*, August 11, https://www.nytimes.com/2015/08/12/upshot/why-did-china-devalue-its-currency-two-big-reasons.html.

4. Zheng, Shi, & Wang, Zhigang (2013). Pricing Efficiency in the Chinese NGM and GM Soybean Futures Market. *China: An International Journal* 11(3): 48–67, https://go.gale.com/ps/i.do?id=-GALE%7CA354661783&sid=googleScholar&v=2.1&it=r&link-access=abs&issn=02197472&p=AONE&sw=w&userGroupName=-nysl_oweb.

Conclusion and Solution

1. Payer, Cheryl (1975). *The Debt Trap: The International Monetary Fund and the Third World* (New York: Monthly Review Press).

2. Shoemaker, Robbin, Harwood, Joy, Rubenstein, Kelly Day, et al. (2001). Economic Issues in Agricultural Biotechnology. USDA Economic Research Service, March 19, https://www.ers.usda.gov/publications/pub-details/?pubid=42313.

3. Bouvard, Véronique, Loomis, Dana, Guyton, Kathryn Z., et al. (2015). Carcinogenicity of Consumption of Red and Processed Meat. *The Lancet Oncology* 16(16):1599–1600, https://doi.org/10.1016/S1470-2045(15)00444-1.

4. Bishop, John (dir.) (2002). *Deconstructing Supper* (Bullfrog Films).

About the Author

 **Omowale Adewale**, born Lawrence James, is from Crown Heights, Brooklyn, NY. During his trip to Lagos, Nigeria, in 2005, he was given the name by his late friend and organizer Moyosore Akojenu. Omowale Adewale means "the son has come home" or "the crown has returned."

Adewale was a teen amateur bodybuilder finalist and two-time collegiate gold medalist at 18. He has competed at boxing, martial arts, and mixed martial arts matches and tournaments since he was 19. Adewale won an amateur boxing belt in mid-30s. He had been vegetarian for four years.

Since the age of seven, Adewale was attracted to political change. He had managed to work at every level of local and state electoral campaign, including as a campaign manager with an above-average success rate without ever graduating from college. He worked in the NYS Assembly for six years.

In 2001, after a year of fostering his vision of an artist union recognizing the mistreatment of artists, Adewale spearheaded the Grassroots Artists MovEment (G.A.ME) with other organizers. Between 2003 and 2006, G.A.ME received significant recognition in the organizational world and music industry, especially from the hip-hop genre. G.A.ME accomplished providing healthcare check-ups to artists for a limited time and helped them understand their contracts within the racist music system. The change they fostered in adopting projects to help young people of color redefine themselves blossoms to this day.

In 2004, Adewale's first published work, "Hip-Hop, Race and Cultural Politics," was featured in the 36th issue of *Socialism & Democracy*. At the behest of Rep. John Conyers, he testified in 2004 and 2006 at the congressional hearing on universal healthcare on behalf of independent artists and low-income communities in need of better access to quality healthcare.

A year after Adewale became vegan in 2013, he helped many people adopt a plant-based lifestyle with his parties in New York City and the #GoVeg2014 campaign. Adewale founded Black VegFest, an Unapologetically Black vegan festival that provides resources for teaching and empowering Black people and creates a space for people of color to convene.

Omowale Adewale is the editor of *Brotha Vegan*, a 2021 anthology published by Lantern Publishing & Media. Along with Nadia Muyeeb, he is the co-owner of Liberation Farm in Sullivan County, NY.

About the Publisher

Lantern Publishing & Media was founded in 2020 to follow and expand on the legacy of Lantern Books—a publishing company started in 1999 on the principles of living with a greater depth and commitment to the preservation of the natural world. Like its predecessor, Lantern Publishing & Media produces books on animal advocacy, veganism, religion, social justice, and psychology and family therapy. Lantern is dedicated to printing in the United States on recycled paper and saving resources in our day-to-day operations. Our titles are also available as e-books and audiobooks.

To catch up on Lantern's publishing program, visit us at www.lanternpm.org.

facebook.com/lanternpm
twitter.com/lanternpm
instagram.com/lanternpm